tipo 00

THE *PASTA* COOKBOOK

tipo 00 THE *PASTA* COOKBOOK

Andreas Papadakis

murdoch books

Sydney | London

CONTENTS

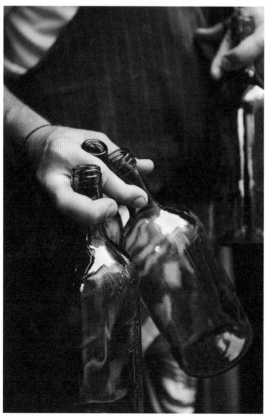

HOW I GOT HERE
A Story in Six Steps

(In which a fit, lean, motorcycle-loving, fine-dining-trained
Greek chef finds success in Australia through pasta)

01: IDENTIFY YOUR PASSION

I was sixteen and still at school in Athens when I started working at my first restaurant. It was a weekend kitchen-hand job that was originally just a way to make some money, but I took to it really quickly and was soon moved on to food prep and then service, working alongside the chefs. I stayed at that restaurant through school and into my architecture degree, before realising that I needed to make a decision about whether I was going to be an architect or a chef. I enrolled in cooking school, then started doing seasonal work on the island of Santorini, a tough gig that involved working seven months straight, with no days off and a double shift every day. It's where I got my work ethic, but it's also where I came to understand that my true passion lay in the kitchen.

02: BROADEN YOUR HORIZONS

Greek food was great, but I wanted to do more. It was the 1990s, French food was really big and Paris was the centre of it, and so I moved to Paris and spent three years there. I learned French, did a culinary course at the Ritz and worked in old-school Michelin Star restaurants. As I'm into motorbikes, on my days off I would ride into Italy, and this was how I got into Italian food. I'd eaten a lot of pasta growing up on Crete with my family, but it was when I was touring around on my bike that pasta really became a big part of me. Then I was offered the chance to run a fine-dining restaurant in Nelson, a small town on New Zealand's South Island, so my wife Anne and I moved there. Obviously it was a culture shock going from Paris to Nelson, but it was also a massive learning curve. I was writing menus, structuring dishes around the place and the produce, working with the seasons. I learned a lot about running a restaurant. A couple of years later, Anne was offered a great job in Melbourne and so we moved again. I landed a job at a fine-dining restaurant and learned more there too – particularly how to deal with difficult situations – but it was starting to dawn on me that this wasn't the kind of cooking I wanted to do any more. And so I left, to put time and thought into how and what I really wanted to cook.

03: BE READY TO CHANGE DIRECTION

It was pretty clear to me I didn't want to do fine dining anymore, but I still loved the idea of restaurants. I loved to source great ingredients and execute and present them well, but I wanted to do that in a more casual environment, one that was fun, hospitable and affordable. I spent a year or two doing pop-up events and consulting. I was putting my style together – what I like to eat and what I like to do, working out who I am as a chef. I ate out a lot, mostly Italian as that was what was still speaking to me, and I discovered a surprisingly massive gap in Italian food in Melbourne. It was difficult to find a decent bowl of pasta that wasn't in an expensive fine dining restaurant. More and more, a pasta restaurant made sense to me.

04: FIND YOUR PEOPLE

Finding the right people to go into business with is vital in any venture, food or otherwise. Luke Skidmore and I had worked together in fine dining, and were keen to work together again. I think we'd arrived at the same point at the same time of no longer being invested in fine dining. We both loved aspects of it but were more interested in the idea of bringing an extra level of quality to everyday dining. Elevating the casual. We discussed lots of different options, including sandwiches, but it became clear pretty quickly that the pasta bar idea was the one that we loved. Luke suggested the name Tipo 00. It was kind of genius. The right name can be half the success. Luke also introduced me to Alberto Fava, who he'd worked with at another Italian restaurant. It was quickly apparent that my skills and Alberto's were really complementary. He knew the fundamentals of what makes a good pasta, and I added the refinement I'd learned from my background. It worked. Even Luke didn't expect the food to be that good from day one. It's all about the right people.

LEFT *Luke, ready for action*
OPPOSITE *With Alberto and Luke outside Tipo*

12

05: LISTEN TO YOUR GUT

For me, Tipo was conceptual for a long time. I had done lots of research, eaten so much pasta, written so many recipes, but when we first opened I still felt like I didn't know exactly what I was doing. But it worked because our team came together really well. Luke and I were nervous because this was the first restaurant either of us had opened and we were sinking a lot of money into it. Luke found the site, which was basically just a concrete shell, but we both agreed that it was the right place, even if it was in a part of the city that wasn't known for having a lot of good restaurants at that time and its kitchen was smaller than ideal. We signed the lease. Luke's sister designed Tipo 00 and his father built it. Even in the lead-up to opening, we were still mulling over whether we should only serve pasta or if we should broaden that out a bit and include things like panini. But we stuck with our instinct and kept the pasta bar idea pretty pure. We also tossed around ideas of when we'd open. I remembered all the times when I'd finished a lunch service in a restaurant and would be wanting something to eat, but it was nearly impossible to find something decent. Then I thought: I'm in the kitchen all day anyway, so why close between lunch and dinner? I figured I liked to eat late lunches so there must be a few other people around who would like to do that too. And if I could serve five or six pastas in these two hours between dinner and lunch, it might add up to fifty covers a week; that would be like an extra service and would help pay the rent. A few months in, we were doing fifty pastas between 3 and 5pm most days, and I realised there were more than a few people like me in Melbourne who were looking for a late lunch. Sometimes you just have to trust your instincts.

06: OPEN AN ALL-DAY PASTA RESTAURANT

But before this rush, we did have some quiet, slightly nerve-wracking days in the first month. Now we sometimes wish we had a larger space, a few more seats, a bigger kitchen. But the balance is about right. We've kept things simple. The techniques we sometimes apply to pasta and pasta sauces often have elements of fine dining, but it's all in service of flavour, not to turn a bowl of pasta into some kind of intellectual exercise. We wanted to feed people well with beautiful ingredients in an atmosphere that was fun and casual. It was an idea that formulated over many years and it's surprising to me how close to our original ideas Tipo has always been. We trusted ourselves. That's how we got here.

How to Make Pasta

We use a lot of different doughs to make our pasta in the restaurant, but this is a good universal recipe. For home cooks, the main thing to note is the dryness of the dough – I believe that many recipes for making pasta at home produce a dough that is too wet. This might make it easier to roll and shape, but it won't have the right strength. If your pasta dough is too wet, once you put the rolled and cut or shaped pasta in boiling water to cook, it quickly takes on the consistency of a dumpling.

At the restaurant, we use a hand-cranked pasta machine that's similar to most household ones, but heavier duty and about double the size. It's worth investing in a quality pasta machine, as cheaper ones are often difficult to work with and won't last the distance. See page 32 for more specific recommendations on pasta machines and other tools.

The *quality of the flour* you use is obviously very important, but equally important is the ratio of the different types of flour. I like to use predominantly '00' flour, the most finely milled type of flour, and semolina flour, in a ratio of 70:30. Regular '00' wheat flour is low in protein, whereas semolina, made from durum wheat, is high in protein. With semolina in the mix, you can reduce the amount of egg yolk needed to bind the dough, and so the pasta will be less rich and eggy. Whole eggs are also included, with the whites adding moisture.

Notice that I give the *quantity of liquid ingredients needed*, including egg and egg yolk as a weight, together with an estimate of roughly how many eggs you'll need to get this exact amount: just crack the eggs into a bowl and lightly mix with a fork before weighing out the amount you need. This is important because weight is more accurate than volume and eggs vary in size so much – adding even a little extra liquid or egg can make a massive difference to your pasta dough.

Be aware that this dough tends to take longer to come together and will have more 'crumbs' when you make it than a regular dough. The crumbs will start off small and then become bigger as you work the dough. When the dough is ready, wrap it in plastic film and let it rest for up to 3 hours at room temperature or, better still, overnight in the fridge, before bringing it back to room temperature.

For rolling the dough, you'll need a good solid pasta machine. The dryness of this dough can make rolling with a smaller machine a bit of a challenge, but the end result will be amazing. What I recommend is having a spray bottle on hand to humidify the dough with a couple of sprays, if necessary.

The pasta machine finalises the mixing as the dough is rolled. On the first pass, it won't be smooth, but the second time it will be better and, depending on the thoroughness of the initial mixing, a third pass through the rollers may be necessary to achieve a smooth dough.

$\rightarrow$

Master pasta dough

MAKES ENOUGH PASTA FOR 4-6

350 g (12 oz) '00' flour
150 g (5½ oz) durum wheat
    semolina flour
1 teaspoon sea salt
65 g (2¼ oz) egg yolk
    (from about 3–4 eggs)
190 g (6¾ oz) whole egg
    (about 4 eggs)

If using an electric mixer, place both flours and the salt in the bowl of a mixer fitted with the dough hook attachment. Make a well in the centre and add the egg yolk and whole egg. (I find it easiest to weigh the egg yolks in a clean bowl first and then add the whole eggs to the same bowl up to the total amount of eggs, which is 255 g (9 oz) for this recipe. The total amount of egg is the important part.) Mix on slow speed for 8–10 minutes, until you start seeing large crumbs forming and the dough starts coming together. Transfer the dough to a clean benchtop and knead by hand until it comes together. Don't expect it to be really smooth, as this is a drier dough – it will come together more and get smoother in the rolling process.

To make the dough by hand, combine both flours and the salt in a mixing bowl. Make a well in the centre and add the egg yolk and whole egg. Mix with a fork until just combined, then transfer to a clean benchtop and knead by hand for 6–8 minutes until the dough comes together.

If the dough seems too dry and won't come together, you can spray it a couple of times with your spray bottle of water – just be careful not to overdo it and make the dough too wet, since it will become more hydrated and softer as it rests.

I like to shape the dough into a roughly rectangular block, rather than a ball, as I find it easier to feed through the pasta machine later. Wrap your dough really well in plastic film, making it as airtight as possible (at the restaurant we use a vacuum sealer).

If you are planning to make your pasta straight away, let the dough rest for at least an hour at room temperature – but ideally refrigerate it overnight, then take it out a couple of hours before rolling and cutting to let it come back to room temperature.

To make the rolling more manageable, it's best to work with a relatively small amount of dough, so divide it in two before you start. (If you are not using all the dough at once, you can refrigerate the rest of it, tightly wrapped, for up to 3 days.)

→

ROLLING AND FOLDING THE DOUGH

Set up the pasta machine on a solid benchtop. Using your hands or a rolling pin, flatten the dough enough that it will go through the widest setting on the pasta machine, then pass it through the rollers two or three times, going down one notch each time. **(1)**

Bring both sides of the dough to the centre, so they meet in the middle, then fold in half to create four layers of dough. **(2)**

Roll the dough through the widest setting again, then repeat the folding and rolling process one more time – but this time bring one third of the dough into the centre, laying it over the middle third, then cover with the last third to create three layers. **(3)**

Flatten the dough again, so that it will go through the widest setting on your machine, then pass it through the rollers, going down one notch at a time; it should be smooth by now and starting to become elastic. Keep going until the pasta sheets are the thickness you need: for filled pasta, you want a $1-1.5$ mm ($1/16$ inch) thickness, and for long and short shapes, $2-3$ mm ($1/8$ inch). **(4)**

CUTTING AND SHAPING THE DOUGH

For long pasta (such as spaghetti and tagliatelle), the sheets are cut into strips using the cutter attachment on your pasta machine (if it has one) or a sharp knife.

For shaped pasta (such as garganelli), the sheets are cut into squares with a pasta wheel and then formed into shapes.

For filled pasta (such as tortelloni and ravioli), the sheets are also cut into squares or circles before being filled and sealed.

And for more rustic kinds of pasta (such as fusilli al ferretto and orecchiette), the dough is not machine-rolled into sheets at all, but simply shaped by hand.

See pages 26–30 for more on pasta shapes, and the individual recipes for specific instructions.

Long Pasta Shapes

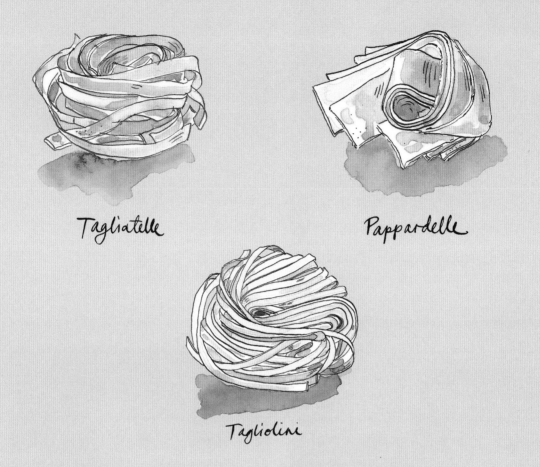

Tagliatelle

Pappardelle

Tagliolini

TAGLIATELLE
Native to Emilia Romagna, long and flat in shape, tagliatelle has a clinginess ideally suited to meaty sauces. We always make it with eggs in the dough. The Bolognese swear by this shape and this shape only for their eponymous tagliatelle al ragu (never spag Bol!).

TAGLIOLINI
Essentially a thinly cut tagliatelle, tagliolini is long, flat and delicately narrow. It can be made simply with just semolina and water or, for a more fulsome roundness, with the addition of eggs. We sometimes add squid ink or saffron.

PAPPARDELLE
This is something like tagliatelle but thicker and wider and made from an especially rich egg dough. It also happens to have become my nickname in the restaurant – perhaps the reason why I'm a touch sentimental about it.

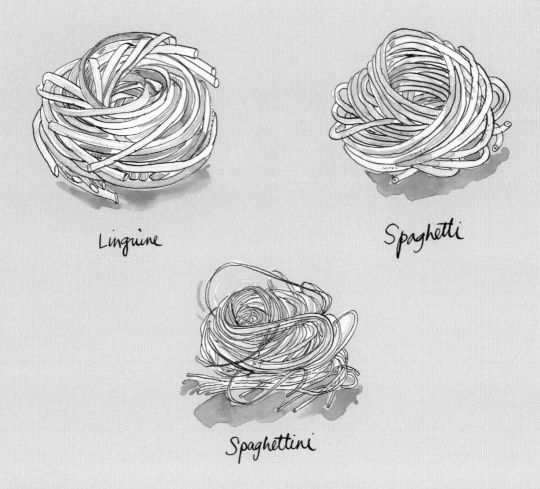

Linguine

Spaghetti

Spaghettini

LINGUINE
From the Italian for 'little tongues', linguine is an extruded pasta – made with a machine that pushes the dough through an attachment to get the desired shape. Most commonly used with seafood sauces, the closest hand-rolled shape to linguine is tagliolini, but linguine has a more rounded shape.

SPAGHETTINI
Far finer than spaghetti, but not quite as light as angel hair, spaghettini has a finer texture that means it cooks faster and takes up more of the sauce. It's a particularly good shape for delicate seafood sauces.

SPAGHETTI
The King of Pasta. Extruded spaghetti emerges rough, textured and with a resistance to the tooth superior to other pastas. See page 58 for more on spaghetti.

Filled and Shaped Pasta

Ravioli

Cappellacci

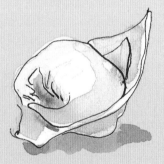

Tortelloni

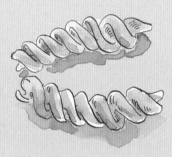

Fusilli al Fero

RAVIOLI
The celebrity filled pasta, either square or round in shape, made from two sheets pressed together and often with fluted or serrated edges.

TORTELLONI
The most recognised of all the filled pasta shapes, tortelloni is made from a single folded over sheet of pasta, with many variations on size and in ways of closing the 'parcel'. It identifies as the larger sibling of tortelli and tortellini.

CAPPELLACCI
Another shape native to Emilia Romagna, cappellacci gets its name from the shape of a hat once commonly worn by locals. At the restaurant, we only use this shape when local pumpkins are in season and we can make the filling from them.

FUSILLI
Fusilli is widely recognised for its spiral shape. We make a handmade version called fusilli al ferretto. It takes its name from the metal skewer that you roll strips of pasta around.

Orecchiette

Cannelloni

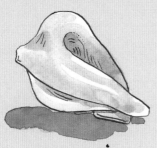

Sorpresine

Paccheri

ORECCHIETTE
The most handmade of the handmade pasta shapes. Rough in texture and rewardingly thick to the bite, orecchiette (named for its ear-like shape) makes for quintessentially simple, fun and delicious eating.

SORPRESINE
This is an open-style ravioli, only folded and without filling. Best used with simple traditional sauces such as butter and sage, tomato and basil or cacio e pepe.

CANNELLONI
Pasta sheets filled or wrapped around a filling in a tube shape and then baked. I only recommend this with a tomato base and a light ricotta filling.

PACCHERI
Thick tubes, not unlike cannelloni, but shorter and thicker. At the restaurant we use different lengths, depending on the sauce.

Filled and Shaped Pasta

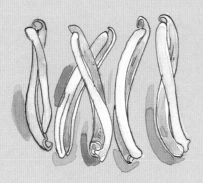

Casarecce

Rigatoni

Garganelli

Gnocchi

CASARECCE
Typically an extruded shape – which is ironic, given that its name means homemade – but a similar version of it can be handmade with a ferretto (a simple square brass stick). Casarecce is specially suited to drier or chunkier, sauce-light recipes, such as a white-based ragu or a chunky Norma.

GARGANELLI
Square sheets wrapped diagonally around a wooden dowel and rolled over a ribbed board. It works well with most ragu or an Amatriciana-style sauce.

RIGATONI
Square sheets wrapped around a wooden dowel and rolled on a ribbed board, which makes grooves that run the length of the tube. Rigatoni is best suited for thicker, more substantial sauces.

GNOCCHI
I'm not sure how I feel about gnocchi as a pasta, but the one we make with a duck ragu is life-changing. And my kids love it.

Pasta-Making Tools

For the purposes of this book, no fancy tools are required. These recommendations cover a range of tools that can enhance the pasta-making experience, from rolling and cutting pasta to mixing the dough and maintaining the right consistency. They cater to both beginners and those with some pasta-making experience.

PASTA MACHINE

There are plenty of good Italian brands of domestic and commercial pasta machine, but I use Imperia. If you'll be making pasta a couple of times a week, I recommend the Imperia 'restaurant' model, which is bigger than the domestic ones and really solid. If you can find a used one, they often go for half price or even less.

MIXER

You can mix your pasta dough by hand, but having a sturdy stand mixer makes life so much easier and neater. I use a KitchenAid both at home and at work.

PASTA BOARD

Rolling pasta on a wooden surface is ideal, as the wood will absorb any excess moisture and pasta cutters work really well on it. There are specific pasta boards, which you can buy pretty cheaply, but any large piece of natural untreated timber that fits on your benchtop will do — just make sure it's sanded smooth to avoid splinters!

DOUGH SCRAPER

Made of plastic or metal, an inexpensive dough scraper is really useful when working pasta dough by hand.

RIBBED GNOCCHI BOARD

This small, hand-held wooden board is used to add the distinctive grooves to rigatoni, garganelli and gnocchi as they are rolled across its ribbed surface.

MATTARELLI

A variety of mini rolling pins, or mattarelli, for different pasta shapes is a great asset. Look online for a set with several rolling pins of different diameter and a brass 'ferretto' (for making fusilli al ferretto).

PASTA CUTTERS

There are some beautiful old-school brass wheel cutters that will last a lifetime, but they are very expensive. I would look for a stainless-steel one at your local restaurant and catering supply shop, which is also a great place to get a set of round and square cutters for filled pasta.

SPRAY BOTTLE

If you have never used a spray bottle when making pasta dough, this will be life-changing. A light spray of water adds just the right amount of moisture to your dough and, if you're making filled pasta, will also help with sealing the edges together properly.

PASTA FOR ONE
A Philosophy

I like pasta. A lot. No real surprise there but, in the early days of Tipo, my business partner Alberto said to me, 'You eat pasta more than anyone I've ever met.' It's true. I'm happy to eat two bowls of pasta every day. But even if you're not cooking (and eating) pasta as regularly as I do, to me it needs to be done right every time. And unwittingly most people cooking pasta at home are not doing it right, because they're cooking it in big batches.

TO COOK PASTA PROPERLY, YOU SHOULD ONLY BE COOKING ONE SERVE AT A TIME.

It's what we do at Tipo and it's why people keep coming back. Here's how we do it.

We make the sauce and put it in the pan with one serve of pasta that's been cooked a little short of al dente.

TO ME, AL DENTE IS A FEELING RATHER THAN A TEXTURE.

It's a hard gig to clearly define the term 'al dente'. For me, it is what separates pasta from noodles, but obviously there is a lot more to it. Literally it means 'to the tooth', a description of the texture of cooked pasta that is firm when bitten, with a slight resistance or chewiness. But I have come to realise that it means different things to different people. Hardcore Italians might like their pasta really crunchy, but fresh pasta made by hand is never going to be like that. The type of pasta, its thickness and its intended use in a dish all contribute to the specific meaning of 'al dente' in each case.

Then we toss the pasta with the sauce, usually for about 45 seconds, but no more than a minute because it can overcook very quickly. Tossing emulsifies the sauce, so it thickens and reaches the right consistency. The pasta not only finishes cooking in the sauce, but also gets coated properly and absorbs the flavours of the sauce.

You can't toss a pan properly if it's overloaded with multiple serves of pasta. There's a heat factor at play too. If you have a big mass of pasta and sauce and you're trying to stir it through (because it's all too large and heavy to toss), the pasta continues to cook and turns gluggy. You lose the lightness and freshness you get when you're cooking one portion of pasta at a time.

I'm not saying that from this point onwards you must only cook individual serves of pasta – I have a young family and I know how hectic life can be, without adding this to the list. In fact, the recipes in the book are designed to make between 2 and 6 servings, so they will work both for everyday meals at home and for when you have people over, but they also include guidance on how to get the best results when making multiple serves of pasta. One important thing to note is that dry pasta will always be more forgiving when you're making multiple serves.

I still wanted to share the Tipo technique, though, so that when you have the time and inclination, you can try it and see what a difference it makes, especially if you are using fresh pasta. It takes a little more planning and adjusting your thinking about everyone eating at exactly the same time (and will mean more washing up), but, believe me, the end result is so much better.

Long Pasta

Spaghetti with king prawns & cavolo nero

The amazing thing about this dish is the prawn sauce, which is a basic Napoli tomato sauce simmered with the flavoured oil from the confit prawn shells and heads. The flavour is sensational.

SERVES 2

4 large or extra-large king
    prawns, 400–500 g
    (14 oz–1 lb 2 oz) in total
150 g (5½ oz) cavolo nero
    (Tuscan kale)
225 g (8 oz) quality
    dried spaghetti – or
    ½ quantity master pasta
    dough (see page 23), cut into
    strips 30 cm (12 inches) long
    and 2 mm (⅟₁₆ inch) wide
olive oil
sea salt

FOR THE SAUCE
50 ml (1½ fl oz) olive oil
prawn heads and shells
    (from preparing the prawns)
1 sprig of thyme
1 sprig of sage
300 ml (10½ fl oz) Napoli tomato
    sauce (see page 219)

TO FINISH
1 large clove of garlic,
    finely chopped
½ long red chilli, finely chopped,
    or more to taste
100 ml (3½ fl oz) dry white wine
squeeze of lemon juice
fennel fronds, to garnish –
    optional

To prepare the prawns, take the head off the body, remove the livery parts under cold running water and reserve the head for the sauce. Peel the shell off the body, leaving only the tail segment, then remove the dark digestive tract that runs the length of the body. Reserve the shells for the sauce as well.

For the sauce, place a saucepan over medium heat, add half the olive oil and the reserved prawn heads and shells and cook really well for 5–6 minutes, stirring so they colour evenly. Add the herbs and Napoli tomato sauce and bring to a slow simmer. Add the remaining olive oil, cover the pan with a lid and cook the sauce over the lowest possible heat for 45 minutes, stirring occasionally to make sure it doesn't catch on the bottom. Pass through a colander with large holes, pushing with the back of a ladle to squeeze the juices out of the prawn heads.

Strip the leaves of the cavolo nero from the stalks and discard the stalks. Wash the leaves and coarsely chop into large pieces, then blanch in boiling salted water for 2 minutes. Drain well and set aside.

To cook the prawns, place a frying pan over medium-low heat. Season the prawns with salt, drizzle with olive oil and cook for 1 minute on each side until just cooked. Remove from the pan and keep warm.

To finish, in the same frying pan, briefly saute the garlic and chilli in olive oil. Deglaze with the wine and simmer until reduced by half, then add the sauce and cavolo nero and bring to a simmer. Season with salt and cook for 2 minutes.

In the meantime, cook the spaghetti in plenty of boiling salted water until al dente, according to the instructions on the package for dried, or 3–4 minutes for fresh.

Drain the spaghetti (reserving some of the pasta water) and add to the sauce. Remove from the heat and toss for 1 minute to coat the pasta. Add the lemon juice and season with salt, if needed, then add just enough of the reserved pasta water to give you the perfect sauce consistency and toss again. Divide the spaghetti and sauce between warmed bowls. Briefly return the prawns to the frying pan, just to warm them through in the residual heat and coat them with the pan juices. Serve on top of the spaghetti and garnish with fennel fronds, if you like.

Squid ink tagliolini with calamari

This has been a signature dish at Tipo since day one. We tried to take it off the menu once, but people kept coming in and asking for it, so it went back on, and it has been there ever since. We use fresh calamari and cut it into the same shape as the tagliolini, then the two tangle together. You should be able to find bottarga and squid ink at any good fishmonger or deli.

SERVES 2

FOR THE PASTA DOUGH
10 g (¼ oz) squid ink
30 g (1 oz) dry white wine
20 g (¾ oz) egg yolk (from 1 egg)
60 g (2¼ oz) whole egg (1 egg)
50 g (1¾ oz) '00' flour
200 g (7 oz) durum wheat semolina flour

FOR THE CALAMARI
1 x 300–400 g (10½–14 oz) calamari, cleaned
1 large clove of garlic, finely chopped
½ long red chilli, finely chopped, or more to taste
about 250 ml (1 cup) quality fish stock
1 tablespoon finely chopped flat-leaf parsley leaves
finely grated zest of ½ lemon
olive oil
sea salt

TO FINISH
bottarga, to serve
2 teaspoons salmon roe, ideally Tasmanian

For the pasta dough, combine the squid ink, wine, egg yolk and whole egg. Now follow the master recipe on page 23, using this squid ink, wine and egg mix (in place of the egg yolk and whole egg) to bring the dough together.

Roll out the dough to 2 mm (1/16 inch) thick, then cut into sheets around 30 cm (12 inches) long and lightly dust with semolina flour. If your pasta machine has a 3–4 mm (1/8 inch) cutter attachment, you can use that to cut the tagliolini, or simply fold the sheets in half and cut into 3–4 mm (1/8 inch) wide strips with a sharp knife. Dust with plenty of semolina flour and leave to dry for several hours.

To prepare the calamari, cut open the body and make sure it is really clean. It will be easier to slice the calamari thinly if you spread it out flat and put it in the freezer until it's almost semi-frozen, about 1 hour. With a sharp knife, cut the calamari body lengthwise into strips as thin as possible and finely chop the tentacles.

Place a large frying pan over medium-low heat, add a generous amount of olive oil and fry the garlic and chilli until translucent, about 1 minute.

Pour in the stock and bring to the boil, then add the calamari, season with salt and simmer for 2–3 minutes until tender.

In the meantime, cook the tagliolini in plenty of boiling salted water until al dente, about 2–3 minutes, depending on how dry the pasta is.

Drain the pasta and add to the calamari. Add the parsley and lemon zest, drizzle with olive oil and toss for 1 minute. The sauce will start getting thicker and darker from the squid ink. Taste for salt and add a little more stock if it seems too dry.

To finish, divide between warmed bowls. Finely grate over a generous amount of bottarga and spoon the salmon roe on top.

Spaghetti with cured rainbow trout, mussels & tomato butter

This is a delicious, refined dish that's unique to Tipo. You won't find anything like it in Italy. For the tomato butter, you'll need to use a dark, ripe tomato, such as a Black Russian. The rainbow trout is not cooked in the sauce, but separately – and gently – then flaked through the sauce as you eat the pasta.

SERVES 2

225 g (8 oz) quality dried spaghetti – or ½ quantity master pasta dough (see page 23), cut into strips 30 cm (12 inches) long and 2 mm (¹⁄₁₆ inch) wide

FOR THE CURED RAINBOW TROUT
50 g (1¾ oz) fine salt
25 g (1 oz) white sugar
2 rainbow trout fillets, skinned and pin-boned

FOR THE MUSSELS
1 tablespoon olive oil
1 clove of garlic
1 sprig of thyme
500 g (1 lb 2 oz) mussels, scrubbed and de-bearded
50 ml (1½ fl oz) dry white wine

FOR THE TOMATO BUTTER
60 g (2¼ oz) unsalted butter
3 anchovy fillets
½ teaspoon fennel seeds
250 g (9 oz) ripe Black Russian tomatoes, grated on a box grater

TO FINISH
1 clove of garlic, finely chopped
½ teaspoon fennel seeds
½ teaspoon chilli flakes
olive oil
squeeze of lemon juice
sea salt
sea herbs, such as purslane, samphire or seablite, if available

To cure the rainbow trout, first make a brine by bringing 500 ml (2 cups) of water, the salt and sugar to the boil and stirring until the salt and sugar has just dissolved. Put the brine in the fridge until completely cold, then submerge the trout in it for 45 minutes, drain and pat dry.

To steam the mussels, place a large saucepan over medium-high heat. Add the olive oil, garlic, thyme, mussels and wine all at once, covering with a lid straightaway to create steam. Cook until the mussels are just open, 2–3 minutes. Pick the mussels out of their shells, then strain the juices through a fine sieve and reserve for the tomato butter.

For the tomato butter, melt the butter with the anchovies and fennel seeds in a saucepan over low heat. Once the anchovies start to break down, add the grated tomatoes and reserved mussel juices. Bring to a simmer, cover with a lid and cook for 45 minutes over the lowest possible heat, stirring occasionally to make sure it doesn't catch on the bottom. Let it cool for 10 minutes, then blend with a stick blender until smooth. Pass through a sieve and set aside.

To finish, place a large frying pan over medium-low heat. Saute the garlic, fennel seeds and chilli flakes in a little olive oil until the garlic is translucent. Add the mussels and tomato butter and bring to a simmer.

Preheat the oven to 70°C (158°F) fan-forced. Generously dress the trout fillets with olive oil and heat in the oven for 5–6 minutes until just warm.

In the meantime, cook the spaghetti in boiling salted water until al dente, according to the instructions on the package for dried, or 3–4 minutes for fresh.

Drain the pasta and add to the frying pan, toss together for 1 minute, then add the lemon juice and taste for salt.

Divide the spaghetti between warmed bowls, placing an trout fillet on top of each one. Finish with some local sea herbs, if you have them.

Saffron tagliolini with spanner crab & zucchini

This is an elegant, ingredient-based dish – there's no saffron in the sauce but heaps in the pasta, and so when you toss them together you get a subtle level of flavour that doesn't overpower the delicate crab meat.

SERVES 2

2 cloves of garlic, finely chopped
1 long red chilli, finely chopped
about 250 ml (1 cup) quality fish stock, plus extra if needed
150 g (5½ oz) raw spanner crab meat, or other white crab meat (cooked or raw)
1 small green zucchini (courgette), seeded core removed, cut into matchsticks
1 tablespoon finely chopped flat-leaf parsley leaves
finely grated zest of ½ lemon
olive oil
sea salt

FOR THE PASTA DOUGH
60 g (2¼ oz) dry white wine
0.25 g (¾ teaspoon) saffron threads
60 g (2¼ oz) whole egg (1 egg)
200 g (7 oz) durum wheat semolina flour
50 g (1¾ oz) '00' flour

For the pasta dough, bring the wine and saffron to the boil in a small saucepan, then remove from the heat, cover and leave to infuse until completely cool before combining with the egg. Now follow the master recipe on page 23, using this saffron-infused wine and egg mix (in place of the egg yolk and whole egg) to bring the dough together.

Roll out the dough to 2 mm ($^1/_{16}$ inch) thick, then cut into sheets about 30 cm (12 inches) long and lightly dust with semolina flour. If your pasta machine has a cutter attachment around 3–4 mm ($^1/_8$ inch) wide, you can use that to cut the tagliolini, or simply fold the sheets in half and cut with a sharp knife. Dust with plenty of semolina flour and leave to dry for several hours.

Place a large frying pan over medium-low heat, then fry the garlic and chili with a generous amount of olive oil until translucent, about 1 minute. Pour in the stock and bring to the boil. Add the crab meat, season with salt and simmer for 2–3 minutes.

In the meantime, cook the tagliolini in plenty of boiling salted water until al dente, about 2–3 minutes, depending on how long the pasta has been drying.

Drain the pasta and add to the frying pan, along with the zucchini, parsley and lemon zest. Toss everything together for 1 minute, then taste for salt, toss again and add some more stock, if needed.

Divide between warmed bowls.

Spaghettini with red mullet & onion-anchovy sauce

I could eat this stylish yet homely pasta every day. It takes a bit of time to pull all the elements together, but you'll be glad you did. The recipe is based on a traditional Venetian bigoli in salsa, for which the sauce is normally slow-cooked onions with salt-cured fish. I make a stock with the red mullet bones, which turn the oil they're cooked in a rich red colour, then make an onion puree with lots of oil and anchovies. If you can't find red mullet, you could use snapper or bream. Whatever fish you use, remember to ask your fishmonger to give you the bones for the stock. And if you don't want to make your own pasta, dried spaghettini works really well here.

SERVES 2

225 g (8 oz) quality dried spaghettini – or ½ quantity master pasta dough (see page 23), cut into strips 30 cm (12 inches) long and 2 mm (¹⁄₁₆ inch) wide
olive oil

FOR THE SAFFRON STOCK
red mullet bones (from filleting the fish)
1 small celery stalk, thinly sliced
½ carrot, thinly sliced
½ fennel bulb, thinly sliced, fronds reserved
1 clove of garlic, crushed
50 ml (1½ fl oz) dry white wine
0.25 g (¾ teaspoon) saffron threads

FOR THE ONION-ANCHOVY SAUCE
2½ tablespoons anchovy oil (from the anchovy tin or jar)
250 g (9 oz) brown onions, thinly sliced
25 g (1 oz) anchovy fillets in olive oil – the best you can get
1 large clove of garlic, finely chopped
½ long red chilli, finely chopped

For the saffron stock, place a non-stick frying pan over medium-high heat. Add a couple of tablespoons of olive oil and fry the mullet bones for 2 minutes on each side, then transfer the bones to a clean saucepan. If needed, add a little more oil to the frying pan, then saute the celery, carrot, fennel and garlic for 3–4 minutes, or until softened. Pour in the white wine, stirring to deglaze, and simmer until the wine has almost completely evaporated. Add the contents of the frying pan to the saucepan, along with the saffron and 500 ml (2 cups) of water. Bring the stock to a simmer and cook for 45 minutes, but do not let it reduce by more than half – you will need about 250 ml (1 cup). Strain the stock through a fine sieve and keep warm while you make the sauce.

For the onion-anchovy sauce, place a small saucepan over medium-low heat. Add the anchovy oil and saute the onions until translucent, about 4–5 minutes. Turn the heat down to low and add the anchovies, then put a lid on the pan and cook until the onions are very soft but still moist, around 20–30 minutes. You may need to add some water if it starts sticking or gets too dry. While it's still hot, blend to a fine puree with a stick blender or food processor, adding a little more water, if necessary.

Place a large frying pan over medium-low heat and fry the garlic and chilli in a generous amount of olive oil until translucent, about 1 minute. Add 250 ml (1 cup) of the saffron stock and 2 generous tablespoons of the onion-anchovy puree and bring to a simmer.

Cook the spaghettini in plenty of boiling salted water until al dente, according to the instructions on the package for dried, or about 3–4 minutes for fresh.

FOR THE RED MULLET
2 x 300–350 g (10½–12 oz)
   red mullet, filleted,
     bones reserved for stock
a little plain flour, if needed

TO FINISH
finely grated zest of ½ lemon
squeeze of lemon juice
reserved fennel fronds,
   a few kept whole for garnish,
   the rest chopped
sea salt

In the meantime, for the red mullet, heat a little olive oil in the cleaned non-stick frying pan and cook the fillets on the skin side for 3–4 minutes until crispy (if your non-stick pan is less than reliable, you may need to lightly flour the skin side of the fish first). I normally cook red mullet on the skin side only, but if you prefer it more cooked, just flip it over and cook on the other side for 10 seconds. Remove from the pan and set aside.

Once the pasta is ready, drain and add to the sauce.

To finish, toss over low heat a few times, then add the lemon zest, lemon juice, chopped fennel fronds and salt to taste. Keep tossing until the sauce coats the pasta really well – you may need to add some more saffron stock if it gets too dry.

Spoon 1–1½ tablespoons of the onion-anchovy sauce into each bowl, then top with half of the pasta, followed by two fillets of red mullet. Garnish with whole fennel fronds.

Pictured overleaf

*Spaghettini with red mullet
& onion-anchovy sauce
(see previous page)*

*Pappardelle with
rabbit ragu & hazelnuts
(see overleaf)*

Pappardelle with rabbit ragu & hazelnuts

Once again, choosing the right ingredients is key. We use farmed rabbits from Gippsland because they are tender and full of flavour, rather than too lean and full of muscle, as wild rabbits can be. Jointing a whole rabbit can be daunting, but no refined butchery skills are needed for this recipe, as the meat all gets picked off the bones once it's cooked — and you could always ask your butcher to cut up the rabbit for you. It's also very important to use the finest hazelnuts in this dish, and the best are from Piedmont. Nothing compares to really good Italian hazelnuts — they're worth the extra effort and cash.

As this ragu uses a whole rabbit, it makes more than you need for two people — in fact, it will serve six generously — but the rest will last in the fridge for 3–4 days, or in the freezer for at least a month. If, on the other hand, you're cooking for more than two, you could increase the quantities of pasta and finishing ingredients accordingly and then complete the dish in several pans, unless you have a really large pan that will comfortably fit the amount of pasta and sauce so they can be tossed properly.

SERVES 2

225 g (8 oz) quality dried pappardelle – or ½ quantity master pasta dough (see page 23), rolled out to 2 mm (1/16 inch) thickness, then cut into strips 30 cm (12 inches) long and 2.5–3 cm (1–1¼ inches) wide, lightly dusted with semolina flour

FOR THE RABBIT RAGU
1 farmed rabbit (about 1.5–2 kg/ 3 lb 5 oz–4 lb 8 oz), cut into 6–8 large pieces
plain flour, for dusting
100 ml (3½ fl oz) olive oil
1 large brown onion, diced
2 cloves of garlic, crushed
6–8 sprigs of marjoram
125 ml (½ cup) dry white wine
1 litre (4 cups) chicken stock
sea salt

For the rabbit ragu, preheat the oven to 150–160°C (300–315°F) fan-forced.

Season the rabbit pieces with salt and dust lightly in flour. Place a heavy-based saucepan over medium heat and saute the rabbit pieces in the olive oil. Cook until golden brown on all sides, then transfer to an ovenproof braising pan.

Next add the onion, garlic and marjoram to the saucepan and cook for 4–5 minutes until the onion is soft and translucent. Add the wine and stir to deglaze, then simmer until reduced by half. Add the stock, bring to a simmer and season with salt.

Pour the contents of the saucepan over the rabbit, cover really tightly with foil and cook in the oven for 1–1½ hours, or until the meat of the back legs is falling off the bone.

Let the rabbit cool down in the sauce, then lift it out and pull the meat off the bones, being careful to remove all the small bones. Return the rabbit meat to the sauce and let it rest for at least 30 more minutes.

TO FINISH
50 g (1¾ oz) unsalted butter
30 g (1 oz) best-quality hazelnuts,
    crushed
30g (⅓ cup) finely
    grated parmesan
1 tablespoon hazelnut oil
    or olive oil
1 tablespoon marjoram leaves
cracked black pepper

LUKE'S WINE MATCHES
For me, the marjoram is what
elevates this simple ragu, hence
I'm looking for something to
enhance that flavour. One of my
favourite options is a verdicchio
from the Marche region of Italy.
The grapes are grown at a high
altitude, which gives the wine
acidity, and close enough to the
Adriatic Sea to gain a maritime
influence. With a little age, the
palate of a classic verdicchio
fleshes out into a fuller-bodied
style of white.

To finish, put a third of the ragu into a large frying pan and bring
to a simmer before adding the butter and most of the hazelnuts.

Cook the pappardelle in plenty of boiling salted water until al dente,
according to the instructions on the package for dried, or about
3–4 minutes for fresh. Drain the pasta and toss in the ragu for
1 minute, adding the parmesan, hazelnut or olive oil and most of
the marjoram leaves. Taste for salt and toss again until the ragu
thickens and coats the pasta.

Serve in warmed bowls, finishing with cracked pepper and the
remaining hazelnuts and marjoram leaves.

Pictured on previous page

Linguine with vongole & smoked cherry tomatoes

For this, I've added smoked cherry tomatoes to a traditional vongole (clam) sauce. The smoke is a great element in itself, but it's well worth taking the extra trouble to peel and then confit the cherry tomatoes in oil, as it gives you an amazing, intense result, even if you decide to skip the smoking part.

SERVES 2

500 g (1 lb 2 oz) clams
2 large cloves of garlic,
    finely chopped
½ long red chilli, finely chopped
2 tablespoons olive oil
125ml (½ cup) dry white wine
6 basil leaves, torn
225 g (8 oz) quality dried
    linguine – or ½ quantity
    master pasta dough (see
    page 23), cut into strips
    30 cm (12 inches) long and
    3 mm (⅛ inch) wide
2 tablespoons finely chopped
    flat-leaf parsley leaves
olive oil
sea salt

FOR THE SMOKED CHERRY TOMATOES
200 g (7 oz) ripe cherry tomatoes
100 ml (3½ fl oz) olive oil
2 tablespoons smoking chips
    (from barbecue suppliers)

To purge the clams of sand and silt, leave them to soak in a bowl of lightly salted cold water for 2 hours.

In the meantime, for the smoked cherry tomatoes, preheat the oven to 90°C (194°F) fan-forced. Remove the skin of the tomatoes by blanching them in water kept at a rolling boil for 20 seconds. Drain and plunge into iced water to stop the cooking, then use your fingers or a small knife to peel off the skins. Put the peeled tomatoes into a small baking dish, pour in the olive oil and season with salt, then cook in the oven for 1½ hours – during this time, the tomatoes should shrink to half their size, get darker and become more concentrated in flavour.

Remove the tomatoes from the oven to smoke them. If you have a smoking gun, inject smoke from the smoking chips directly into the dish of tomatoes, cover with foil and leave the tomatoes to absorb the smoke for 20 minutes, then repeat one more time. If you don't have a smoking gun, light half of the smoking chips in a small metal container and, as soon the flame subsides and the chips start smoking, carefully put the metal container into the dish with the tomatoes, cover and leave to smoke for 20 minutes, then repeat with the other half of the smoking chips.

To cook the clams, place a large frying pan over medium heat and fry the garlic and chilli in the olive oil until the garlic is translucent, about 1 minute. Add the clams and wine, cover with a lid and cook for 2–3 minutes or until the clams are just open. Add the tomatoes and half the basil and cook for 3 more minutes, then season with salt to taste.

Cook the linguine in plenty of boiling salted water until al dente, according to the instructions on the package for dried, or about 3–4 minutes for fresh.

Drain the pasta (reserving some of the pasta water) and add to the frying pan, then toss for 1 minute before adding the parsley and the remaining basil. Taste for salt, then toss again until the sauce thickens and coats the pasta, adding some of the reserved pasta water, if needed.

Serve in warmed bowls.

Why SPAGHETTI *is the* KING *of* PASTA

For me, spaghetti is the King of Pasta. It's not easy to explain why, but there's something about eating spaghetti that offers a particular sense of satisfaction. I think it's because al dente spaghetti is unique; its shape and size give the perfect combination of soft on the outside and magical chewiness on the inside.

When I cook spaghetti at home, I use dried pasta, the artisanal kind that's made with a mix of quality durum semolina and extruded through old bronze dies, then dried very slowly. Extruded spaghetti comes out differently from pasta from a pasta machine: it emerges porous, rough and textured – unlike long flat pasta, such as pappardelle, or round hollow pasta, such as paccheri, with their smoother, silkier texture.

You eat spaghetti in a different way from other pasta too. When you wrap spaghetti around your fork and eat a mouthful of it (as opposed to spiking three or four rigatoni at a time), it means you get the complete combination of the dish all at once. With other pasta shapes, it's a different, slower way of eating. The dish is off the heat for longer and that will change the essence of the sauce. It's a unique phenomenon in terms of eating pasta. There's nothing else quite like spaghetti. I enjoy it with everything from a carbonara (see page 144) to my midnight spaghetti (see page 156) or an indulgent seafood sauce, such as the prawn one on page 40.

At Tipo we extrude all our pasta in-house, including our spaghetti; it's our specialty. We manipulate and change the dough recipes too, in order to make each pasta best suit each particular sauce. It was essential to me that all our pasta be made in-house. It works for us in a commercial kitchen with experienced chefs and the correct equipment, but it can be pretty hard to replicate in a home kitchen, not just because of the extruding process but because of the drying of the spaghetti. Dry it too much and it becomes brittle, not enough and it loses the attractive textures that make the more laborious extruding process worth the effort.

So what I'm saying here is: you can't really make spaghetti like this at home. There are versions you can try, such as spaghetti alla chitarra or tonnarelli, but those are more of a square pasta and so don't have the same qualities as the rounded extruded kind. My advice is to buy the best-quality dried spaghetti you can afford, or else track down some freshly extruded spaghetti from a local deli or pasta specialist.

I love fresh pasta. But I also love dried pasta. They are both very different and very beautiful and unique in their own way, so there should be no thought of one being superior to the other. It's more about choosing what goes best with the sauce you're planning to serve. But for the ultimate pasta experience, the one for me that cannot be replicated, spaghetti will always be the king.

Spaghetti with marron & finger lime

The marron and finger lime in this recipe make it distinctively Australian; cooked lobster, yabbies or Moreton Bay bugs make good alternatives if marron is hard to get. Colatura di alici is essentially the Italian equivalent of fish sauce, made by fermenting salted anchovies. Although there are a few elements here, if you have herb oil and fish stock on hand (or make them in advance), this refined dish is pretty simple. As the marron flesh is very delicate, you cook that separately, so it doesn't get overcooked, and then serve it on top with the finger lime dressing.

SERVES 2

1 live marron, about 300–400 g (10½–14 oz)
225 g (8 oz) quality dried spaghetti – or ½ quantity master pasta dough (see page 23), cut into strips 30 cm (12 inches) long and 2 mm (1⁄16 inch) wide

FOR THE SAUCE
1 small fennel bulb (about 150 g/5½ oz), thinly sliced, ideally using a mandoline
2 tablespoons olive oil
250 ml (1 cup) fish stock, plus extra if needed
50 g (1¾ oz) unsalted butter
70 ml (2¼ fl oz) herb oil (see page 206)
1 tablespoon colatura di alici
juice of ½ lemon
sea salt

FOR THE FINGER LIME DRESSING
1 finger lime
1 tablespoon colatura di alici
2 tablespoons herb oil (see page 206)
squeeze of lemon juice

To prepare the marron, chill it in the freezer for 30 minutes to 'put it to sleep'. Meanwhile, bring a large saucepan of well-salted water to the boil.

Take the marron out of the freezer, lay it on a chopping board and insert a knife between the eyes, cutting right down through the head. Put the marron into the boiling water and cook for 4–5 minutes. Take it out and let it cool, then split it in half lengthwise with a sharp knife. Clean all the impurities from the head under cold running water and remove the dark digestive tract from the tail.

For the sauce, place a frying pan over medium-low heat and sweat down the fennel in the olive oil for 5–6 minutes until tender – you don't want any colour. Add the stock, bring to the boil and simmer for 4 minutes, then add the butter and herb oil and stir to emulsify. Season with the colatura di alici, lemon juice and salt. The balance of colatura and lemon is based on personal taste, but I go heavy on the colatura and just offset the saltiness with lemon juice.

For the finger lime dressing, cut the finger lime in half and roll on a chopping board to extract the pearls, discarding any seeds. In a small bowl, use a fork to mix together the finger lime pearls, colatura di alici, herb oil and lemon juice.

Cook the spaghetti in plenty of boiling salted water until al dente, according to the instructions on the package for dried, or about 3–4 minutes for fresh.

In the meantime, gently reheat the marron in the sauce for a minute or two, then set aside on a plate.

Drain the pasta and add to the sauce, then toss for 1 minute until the sauce coats the pasta really well, adding more stock as needed. Taste for seasoning and adjust with salt or lemon juice, if necessary. Serve in warmed bowls, with half a marron on each. Spoon the dressing generously over the marron and spaghetti.

Juniper pappardelle with wild boar ragu

This is a similar recipe to our Bolognese (see page 136), the obvious difference being the wild boar meat, which brings with it a more intense and gamey sauce. The pasta is flavoured with juniper and raspberry, so it's dark and acidic and cuts through the fattiness of the boar; it would work equally beautifully with other game meats, such as venison, wallaby or kangaroo.

The ragu here makes more than you need for two people – in fact, it will serve six generously – but the rest will last in the fridge for 3–4 days, or in the freezer for at least a month. If, on the other hand, you're cooking for more than two, you could increase the quantities of pasta and finishing ingredients accordingly and then complete the dish in several pans, unless you have a really large pan that will comfortably fit the amount of pasta and sauce so they can be tossed properly.

SERVES 2

FOR THE PASTA DOUGH
40 g (1½ oz) egg yolk
   (from about 2–3 eggs)
50 g (1¾ oz) whole egg
   (from 1 egg)
55 g (2 oz) raspberries
1½ heaped teaspoons juniper
   berries, finely ground
200 g (7 oz) '00' flour
100 g (3½ oz) durum wheat
   semolina flour

For the pasta dough, first blend the egg yolk and whole egg with the raspberries and ground juniper until smooth, then pass through a fine sieve. Weigh the liquid and add enough water to make it up to 145 g (5¼ oz). Now follow the master recipe on page 23, using this egg, raspberry and juniper liquid (in place of the egg yolk and whole egg) to bring the dough together.

Roll out the pasta dough to 2 mm (¹⁄₁₆ inch) thick, then cut into sheets around 30 cm (12 inches) long and lightly dust with semolina flour. Fold the sheets in half, then cut into 2.5–3 cm (¾–1¼ inch) wide strips with a sharp knife. Dust with plenty of semolina flour and let it dry for a couple of hours.

For the wild boar ragu, place a large heavy-based saucepan over medium-high heat and add most of the oil. When it is hot, add the meat and brown it for about 5 minutes until it starts caramelising. Be careful not to overcrowd the pan or the meat will stew instead of searing. If your pan is not big enough to comfortably caramelise this amount of meat, it is better to do in two or more batches. Remove the meat with a slotted spoon, so the rendered fats stay in the pan.

Once all the meat is browned, reduce the heat to medium-low, add the onion, carrot, celery and garlic and cook until soft, at least 6-8 minutes. You may need to add more oil, depending on how much fat has rendered from the meat. Slowly cooking this 'soffritto' adds depth of flavour to the sauce.

FOR THE WILD BOAR RAGU

100 ml (3½ fl oz) olive oil
1 kg (2 lb 4 oz) wild boar
   shoulder, half coarsely
   minced and half cut into
   1.5 cm (⅝ inch) cubes
100 g (3½ oz) pork back fat (you
   may need to order this ahead),
   cut into 1 cm (½ inch) cubes
1 brown onion, diced
1 carrot, diced
2 celery stalks, diced
2 cloves of garlic, finely chopped
160 g (5¾ oz) tomato paste
   (concentrated puree)
400 ml (14 fl oz) red wine
600 ml (21 fl oz) chicken stock,
   plus extra if needed
2 juniper berries
1 allspice berry
sea salt and freshly
   ground pepper

TO FINISH

50 g (1¾ oz) unsalted butter
handful of flat-leaf parsley
   leaves, finely chopped
generous drizzle of olive oil
50 g (½ cup) finely
   grated parmesan
cracked black pepper

Return the meat to the pan, along with the tomato paste, and cook for 2–3 minutes. Pour in the wine, stirring to deglaze, then simmer until the wine has almost completely reduced. Add the stock and spices and season with salt and pepper. Cover with a lid and cook over low heat for 1–1½ hours, or until the meat is very tender.

To finish, put a third of the ragu into a large frying pan and bring to a simmer, then stir in the butter.

In the meantime, cook the pappardelle in plenty of boiling salted water until al dente, about 3–4 minutes.

Drain the pasta (reserving some of the pasta water) and add to the ragu in the frying pan, then toss together for 1 minute, making sure the pasta is well coated with the sauce. If it seems too dry, add some of the reserved pasta water or more chicken stock. Finally, stir through the parsley.

Serve in warmed bowls, with a generous drizzle of olive oil, the grated parmesan and some cracked pepper.

Tagliatelle with rabbit, olives & oregano

This is a fairly traditional Mediterranean rabbit ragu, being tomato based and beautifully flavoured with oregano. As this ragu uses a whole rabbit (you can always ask the butcher to cut it up for you), it makes more than you need for two people – in fact, it will serve six generously – but the rest will last in the fridge for 3–4 days, or in the freezer for at least a month. If, on the other hand, you're cooking for more than two, you could increase the quantities of pasta and finishing ingredients accordingly and then complete the dish in several pans, unless you have a really large pan that will comfortably fit the amount of pasta and sauce so they can be tossed properly.

SERVES 2

225 g (8 oz) dried tagliatelle – or 240 g (8½ oz) master pasta dough (see page 23), rolled out to 3 mm (⅛ inch) thickness, then cut into strips 30 cm (12 inches) long and 1.5 cm (⅝ inch) wide, lightly dusted with semolina flour

FOR THE RABBIT RAGU
1 farmed rabbit, about 1.5–2 kg (3 lb 5 oz–4 lb 8 oz), cut into 6–8 large pieces
plain flour, for dusting
100 ml (3½ fl oz) olive oil
1 brown onion, diced
1 carrot, diced
2 cloves of garlic, crushed
75 g (2½ oz) mixed olives, pitted and chopped
100 g (3½ oz) tomato paste (concentrated puree)
125 ml (½ cup) dry white wine
1 litre (4 cups) chicken stock
2 tablespoons dried oregano, ideally Sicilian
sea salt

TO FINISH
50 g (1¾ oz) unsalted butter
handful of flat-leaf parsley leaves, finely chopped
50 g (½ cup) finely grated parmesan
cracked black pepper

Preheat the oven to 150–160°C (300–315°F) fan-forced.

For the rabbit ragu, season the rabbit with salt and dust lightly in flour. Place a heavy-based saucepan over medium heat and saute the rabbit pieces in the olive oil. Cook until golden brown on all sides, then transfer to an ovenproof braising pan.

Next add the onion, carrot and garlic to the saucepan and cook for 4–5 minutes until the onion is soft and translucent, then add the olives and tomato paste and cook over low heat for 2 minutes. Pour in the wine and stir to deglaze, then simmer until reduced by half. Add the stock and oregano, bring to a simmer and season with salt.

Pour the contents of the saucepan over the rabbit, cover really tightly with foil and cook in the oven for 1–1½ hours, or until the meat of the back legs is falling off the bone.

Let the rabbit cool down in the ragu, then lift out and pull the meat off the bones, being careful to remove all the small bones. Return the rabbit meat to the ragu and let it rest for at least 30 more minutes.

Cook the tagliatelle in plenty of boiling salted water until al dente, according to the instructions on the package for dried, or about 3–4 minutes for fresh.

To finish, put a third of the ragu into a large frying pan and bring to a simmer, then stir in the butter.

Drain the pasta and toss with the ragu in the frying pan for 1 minute, adding the parsley and most of the parmesan. Taste for salt and toss again until the ragu thickens and coats the pasta.

Serve in warmed bowls, finishing with the remaining parmesan and some cracked pepper.

Pappardelle with braised wagyu & confit chilli

We use Sher wagyu neck for this, which is an amazing product, but any braising cut of beef works well, as the meat is cooked slowly in the oven until it falls apart. Another layer of flavour comes from the confit chilli, which adds a sweet spicy note rather than a hot one.

The confit chilli and slow-cooked ragu here make more than you need for two people – in fact, they will serve six generously – but the rest will last in the fridge for 3–4 days, or in the freezer for at least a month. If, on the other hand, you're cooking for more than two, you could increase the quantities of pasta and finishing ingredients accordingly and then complete the dish in several pans, unless you have a really large pan that will comfortably fit the amount of pasta and sauce so they can be tossed properly.

SERVES 2

225 g (8 oz) quality dried pappardelle – or ½ quantity master pasta dough (see page 23), rolled out to 3 mm (⅛ inch) thickness, then cut into strips 30 cm (12 inches) long and 2 cm (¾ inch) wide, lightly dusted with semolina flour

FOR THE BRAISED BEEF
750 g (1 lb 10 oz) beef neck or shin, trimmed of the majority of excess fat and cut into 6–8 cm (2½ –3¼ inch) chunks
2½ tablespoons olive oil
1 small brown onion, diced
2 cloves of garlic, crushed
1 small bay leaf
1 sprig of rosemary
2 sprigs of thyme
2 sprigs of sage
200 ml (7 fl oz) dry white wine
400 g (14 oz) tin of peeled tomatoes, preferably Italian
sea salt and freshly ground pepper

Preheat the oven to 150–160°C (300–315°F) fan-forced.

For the braised beef, season the meat with salt and pepper. Place a heavy-based saucepan over medium heat and saute the meat in the olive oil until golden brown on all sides, then transfer to an ovenproof braising pan.

Next add the onion, garlic and herbs to the saucepan and cook for 4–5 minutes until the onion is soft and translucent. Pour in the wine and stir to deglaze, then simmer until reduced by half. Add the tomatoes, bring to a simmer and season with salt.

Pour the contents of the saucepan over the beef, cover really tightly with foil and cook in the oven for 2½–3 hours, or until the meat is falling apart.

Meanwhile, make the confit chilli. In a very small heavy-based saucepan, sweat the shallot with a third of the oil for about 3–4 minutes until soft. Add the chillies and tomato paste and cook for 1 more minute, then add the remaining oil, season with salt and cook on the lowest possible heat for 20–30 minutes – the time needed will depend on how low the heat on your stove goes. When it's ready, it should have a relish-like consistency.

Let the meat cool down in the ragu, then lift it out and break it down into smaller, bite-size pieces. Remove the herb stalks from the ragu and discard. Return the meat to the ragu and let it rest for at least 30 minutes.

Cook the pappardelle in plenty of boiling salted water until al dente, according to the instructions on the package for dried, or about 3–4 minutes for fresh.

FOR THE CONFIT CHILLI
100 g (3½ oz) shallots,
    finely diced
75 ml (2½ fl oz) vegetable oil
    or olive oil
50 g (1¾ oz) long red chillies,
    coarsely chopped into
    1 cm (½ inch) pieces
40 g (1½ oz) tomato paste
    (concentrated puree)

TO FINISH
50 g (1¾ oz) unsalted butter
1 tablespoon flat-leaf parsley
    leaves, finely chopped
30 g (⅓ cup) finely grated
    parmesan

To finish, put a third of the ragu into a large frying pan and bring to a simmer, then stir in the butter and 2–3 tablespoons of the confit chilli, depending on how hot the chillies are.

Drain the pasta and toss with the ragu in the frying pan for 1 minute, adding the parsley and most of the parmesan. Taste for salt and toss again until the ragu thickens and coats the pasta.

Serve in warmed bowls, finishing with the remaining parmesan.

Pictured overleaf

*Pappardelle with braised
wagyu and confit chilli
(see previous page)*

Pasta, Filled *and* Shaped

Asparagus ravioli with parmesan cream

This ravioli combines a cacio e pepe, bechamel-style sauce with thin slices of just-cooked asparagus. If you like, you can save the tips of the asparagus to garnish the dish before serving.

SERVES 4

1 quantity master pasta dough (see page 23), rolled into two sheets 1–1.5 mm (1/16 inch) thick, one a little longer than the other – try to use the whole width of the rollers on your pasta machine, at least 12 cm (4½ inches), to avoid too much wastage

FOR THE FILLING

50 g (1¾ oz) unsalted butter
1 shallot, finely diced
50 g (1¾ oz) plain (all-purpose) flour
250 ml (1 cup) whole milk, warmed
200 g (7 oz) asparagus, stalks thinly sliced – and tips reserved for garnish, if desired
25 g (¼ cup) finely grated parmesan

FOR THE PARMESAN CREAM

100 g (1 cup) finely grated parmesan
125 ml (½ cup) chicken or vegetable stock

To make the filling, melt the butter in a saucepan and cook the shallot until translucent. Add the flour and cook for 3–4 minutes over low heat, stirring with a wooden spoon. Gradually whisk in the warm milk until smooth, then cook for 10 minutes over the lowest possible heat to thicken, stirring to avoid the sauce catching on the bottom.

Add the sliced asparagus and stir for about a minute – you don't want to cook the asparagus too much or it will release all its liquid and make the filling too runny. Stir in the parmesan and season with salt and a lot of pepper. Transfer the filling to a baking tray or dish and cover with plastic film, pressing it directly onto the surface to prevent a skin forming, then leave in the fridge to cool completely.

For the ravioli, place the pasta sheets on a lightly floured surface. Starting with the shorter sheet, use a piping bag or a spoon to place heaped-tablespoon-sized mounds of the filling along the centre of the sheet, spacing them about 4 cm (1½ inches) apart. Lightly brush or spray around the filling with a little water to help seal, then lay the longer pasta sheet over the top, trying to match up the ends of the two pasta sheets.

Using the blunt side of a 4 cm (1½ inch) round pastry cutter, gently press around the filling to remove as much air as possible. With your fingers, gently press on the dough around the filling to seal and remove any remaining air bubbles. Continue doing this from one side of the sheet to the other, then use an 8–9 cm (3¼–3½ inch) round cutter to cut out the ravioli, making sure the mound of filling is exactly in the centre of each one. Set the finished ravioli aside on a well-floured surface while you make the parmesan cream.

For the parmesan cream, put the parmesan into a small heatproof bowl. Heat the stock to just below simmering point, 90°C (194°F), and pour it over the parmesan, then blend with a stick blender until smooth. Cover with plastic film, pressing it directly onto the surface to prevent a skin forming, and keep warm until needed.

Cook the ravioli in plenty of boiling salted water for 3–4 minutes, or until al dente.

TO FINISH

100 g (3½ oz) unsalted
    butter, diced
1 tablespoon finely
    chopped sage leaves
250 ml (1 cup) chicken or
    vegetable stock, warmed
2–3 tablespoons finely
    grated parmesan
sea salt and freshly
    ground pepper

In the meantime, to finish, place a large frying pan over medium-high heat. When it's hot, add the butter – it should start foaming straight away – and cook until golden brown and starting to smell nutty. Add the reserved asparagus tips, if using, the sage and a small ladle of the stock, then season with salt and stir well, adding more stock, a ladle at a time until the sauce has emulsified.

When the ravioli are done, use a slotted spoon to carefully lift them out of the water and transfer them to the frying pan. Gently toss over low heat to make sure they are well coated with the sauce. Add the parmesan and keep tossing until the sauce is thick and smooth, adjusting with a little of the pasta water, if necessary.

Serve on warmed plates, finishing with a few spoonfuls of the parmesan cream.

Pictured overleaf

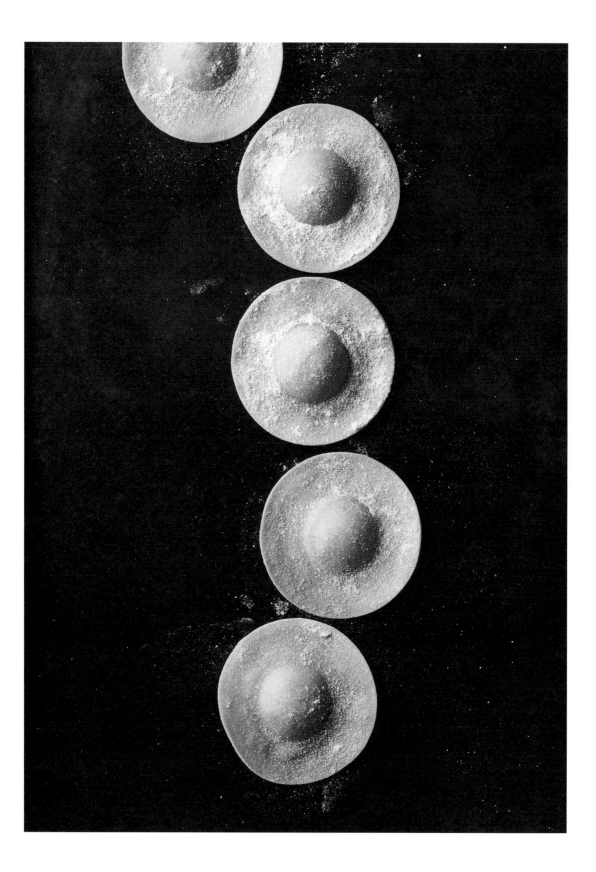

*Asparagus ravioli
with parmesan cream
(see previous page)*

Cocoa paccheri with pine mushrooms & pine nuts

This is a strictly seasonal dish, because the pine mushrooms are non-negotiable. In Australia, where the pine mushroom season is pretty long, you'll often find them at farmers' markets. For this recipe, I make the paccheri longer than traditionally shaped ones – almost as long as cannelloni – and I also add cocoa to the dough, which gives it a lot of depth, and a chocolatey flavour that works beautifully with the earthy flavour of the mushrooms.

SERVES 4

300 g (10½ oz) pine mushrooms
80 g (2¾ oz) unsalted butter
2 tablespoons pine nuts,
    lightly toasted
4 cloves of garlic, finely chopped
2 tablespoons marjoram leaves
350 ml (12 fl oz) vegetable or
    chicken stock, warmed, plus
    extra if needed
80 g (¾ cup) finely
    grated parmesan
sea salt and freshly
    ground pepper

FOR THE PASTA DOUGH
10 g (¼ oz) Dutch-process
    cocoa powder
340 g (11¾ oz) '00' flour
150 g (5½ oz) durum wheat
    semolina flour
1 teaspoon sea salt
65 g (2¼ oz) egg yolk
    (from about 3–4 eggs)
175 g (6 oz) whole egg
    (about 3–4 eggs)

To make the pasta dough, follow the master recipe on page 23, combining the cocoa powder with the flours and salt before you start mixing. Roll the dough into 2–3 mm (⅛ inch) thick sheets.

To shape the paccheri, I use a special cannelloni rolling pin that's about 2.5 cm (1 inch) in diameter, but you can improvise with a similar-sized rolling pin or length of wooden dowel. Lay out the pasta sheets on a lightly floured workbench or wooden board. Cut a rectangle of pasta 9 cm (3½ inches) long and 7 cm (2¾ inches) wide, then check that when you roll it around your rolling pin, starting with one of the longer sides, it just overlaps by 3–4 mm (⅛ inch) – you may need to adjust the size of the rectangle, based on the thickness of your rolling pin. Once you get the size right, cut the pasta sheets into rectangles.

Lightly brush the front edge of a pasta rectangle with water and wrap it around the rolling pin, pressing down firmly where the two edges meet. Gently pull the paccheri off the rolling pin and place it upright on the work surface so it holds its shape. Repeat until all the paccheri are made.

Prepare the pine mushrooms only when you are ready to cook, as they oxidise very quickly when cut and exposed to the air. To clean them, use either a brush or a damp cloth to gently remove any dirt; do not be tempted to rinse them with water. Slice the mushrooms into 1 cm (½ inch) thick slices.

You'll need a very large frying pan for this, or you can use two, dividing the ingredients evenly between them – it's vital that you have plenty of room to toss the pasta through the sauce later on. Place your pan or pans over medium heat and saute the mushrooms in a little olive oil for 2 minutes until they start to soften. Add the butter and pine nuts and season with salt. Turn the heat down to low and continue cooking for 1 more minute, then add the garlic and marjoram and cook until the garlic starts to brown. Pour in the stock, stirring to deglaze, then leave to simmer over very low heat while you cook the pasta.

In the meantime, cook the paccheri in plenty of boiling salted water until al dente, about 3–4 minutes.

Drain the pasta (reserving some of the pasta water) and add to the frying pan, then toss thoroughly. Add the parmesan and keep tossing until the sauce is very well emulsified. Add some stock or reserved pasta water if it starts getting too dry, then taste for salt.

Serve in warmed bowls, arranging the paccheri along the centre with the mushrooms and pine nuts on top and the sauce spooned over. Finish with freshly ground pepper.

Pictured overleaf; paccheri-making process shown on following pages

LUKE'S WINE MATCHES

In choosing a wine to go with this dish, I want to play on the umami notes of the cocoa and mushrooms. The fruit and earth elements in a gamay are great for this. Traditionally a wine from the Beaujolais region of France, the few examples of gamay now popping up in New World wine regions could work equally well here.

Cocoa paccheri with pine mushrooms & pine nuts (see previous page)

PASTA, FILLED AND SHAPED

PASTA, FILLED AND SHAPED

Paccheri with rabbit ragu & nettle oil

I always use farmed rabbits for making rabbit ragu, as they're bigger and their meat is sweeter and easier to cook. Wild rabbits are very lean, can take hours to cook and their flavour is more gamey; they're often cheaper, but you get what you pay for with a farmed rabbit. If you have a mincer, you can mince the rabbit meat and pork fat for the ragu yourself, using a 6–8 mm (¼–⅜ inch) die. Boning a rabbit can be time consuming but, as the meat is going to be minced anyway, it doesn't need to be neatly done – just try to remove as much meat as possible using your knife, and if you see that you have left too much behind, scrape it from the bones with a spoon. If you end up with a little less than the amount needed for the ragu, then slightly reduce the other ingredients as well to keep the balance right.

The ragu makes more than you need for two – in fact, it will serve six generously – but the rest will last in the fridge for 3–4 days, or in the freezer for at least a month. If, on the other hand, you're cooking for more than two, you could increase the quantities of pasta and finishing ingredients accordingly and then complete the dish in several pans, unless you have a really large pan that will comfortably fit the amount of pasta and sauce so they can be tossed and emulsified properly.

SERVES 2

½ quantity master pasta dough (see page 23), rolled into sheets 2–3 mm (⅛ inch) thick

To marinate the meat for the rabbit ragu, put the garlic into a small saucepan and cover with cold water. Bring to the boil, then drain in a fine sieve and rinse under cold running water to cool it down. Mix the meat and fat (if using) with the cooked garlic, salt, pepper, sherry or vermouth and thyme. Leave to marinate in the fridge for at least 3–4 hours, but ideally overnight.

For the paccheri, lay out the pasta sheets on a lightly floured workbench or wooden board. Cut a strip of pasta 9 cm (3½ inches) long and 3 cm (1¼ inches) wide, then check that when you roll it around your rolling pin it just overlaps by 3–4 mm (⅛ inch) – you may need to adjust the size of the strip, based on the thickness of your rolling pin. Once you get the size right, cut the pasta sheets into strips.

Lightly brush the front edge of a pasta strip with water and wrap it around the rolling pin, pressing down firmly where the two edges meet. Gently pull the paccheri off the rolling pin and place it upright on the work surface so it holds its shape. Repeat until all the paccheri are made, then leave to dry for 1–2 hours while you cook the ragu.

FOR THE RABBIT RAGU

5 cloves of garlic, finely chopped

1.5 kg (3 lb 5 oz) minced rabbit meat – ask your butcher to bone and coarsely mince a 2–2.25 kg (4 lb 8 oz–5 lb) farmed rabbit for you

300 g (10½ oz) minced pork back fat – optional

30 g (1 oz) fine salt

10 g (¼ oz) freshly ground pepper

100 ml (3½ fl oz) dry sherry or vermouth

3 teaspoons thyme leaves

3–4 tablespoons olive oil

2 large shallots, finely diced

300 ml (10½ fl oz) dry white wine

1.5 litres (6 cups) stock – you can either use chicken stock or make a stock from the rabbit bones, following the chicken stock method on page 216

TO FINISH

50 g (1¾ oz) unsalted butter

60 ml (¼ cup) nettle oil (see page 207)

35 g (⅓ cup) finely grated parmesan

To make the ragu, drain off any excess marinade from the meat and fat. Preheat a large heavy-based saucepan over medium-high heat. Add the olive oil and cook the meat and fat until brown – if your pan isn't big enough to fit it all comfortably, do this in several batches. Return all the browned meat and fat to the pan and lower the heat, then add the shallot and saute until soft. Add the white wine, stirring to deglaze, then simmer until reduced by half. Pour in the stock and let the ragu simmer for 30 minutes.

Cook the paccheri in plenty of boiling salted water until al dente, about 3–4 minutes, depending on how long the pasta has been drying for.

Meanwhile, to finish, bring a third of the ragu to a simmer in a large frying pan. Add the butter and nettle oil and stir to emulsify, adding a little more stock or water from the pasta pan if it seems too dry.

Drain the pasta and add it to the frying pan, then toss thoroughly, making sure it is well coated with the ragu. Add the parmesan and keep tossing until the cheese has emulsified with the sauce.

Serve in warmed bowls.

Pictured overleaf

Paccheri with rabbit ragu & nettle oil (see previous page)

Gnocchi with duck & porcini ragu (see overleaf)

Gnocchi with duck & porcini ragu

This is another dish that has been on the menu at Tipo 00 from day one. We use corn-fed duck legs for the ragu. The secret to our gnocchi, aside from using Sebago or Russet Burbank potatoes, is that we make them with cold potato: we cook the potatoes, peel them while they're hot and pass them through a drum sieve, so the potato is very fluffy, and then cool it in the fridge. The cold potato absorbs the flour better and doesn't become gluey, as hot potato sometimes does. The dish is finished with pecorino pepato, sheep's milk cheese studded with whole peppercorns. If you can't find it, you could use a good pecorino romano and some cracked black pepper instead.

The gnocchi and ragu here both make more than you need for two people – in fact, they will serve six – but the rest can be kept for another time. If, on the other hand, you're cooking for more than two, you could increase the quantities of gnocchi and finishing ingredients accordingly and then complete the dish in several pans, unless you have a really large pan that will comfortably fit the amount of gnocchi and sauce so they can be tossed properly.

SERVES 2

FOR THE DUCK RAGU
6 duck legs, preferably corn-fed
1 carrot, diced
1 brown onion, diced
2 large cloves of garlic,
    finely chopped
10 g (¼ oz) dried porcini,
    soaked in 250 ml (1 cup) warm
    water for about 15 minutes
100 g (3½ oz) tomato paste
    (concentrated puree)
125 ml (½ cup) dry white wine
750 ml (3 cups) chicken stock
2 sprigs of sage
1 sprig of thyme
1 bay leaf
sea salt

For the duck ragu, take the duck legs out of the fridge about an hour beforehand, season with salt and allow to come to room temperature.

Preheat the oven to 150°C (300°F) fan-forced.

Place a large heavy-based saucepan over medium heat. When it is hot, add the duck legs, skin side down, to render the fat, and cook until golden brown, about 5–6 minutes. Turn the legs over and cook on the other side for 2 minutes, then transfer to an ovenproof braising pan.

Next add the carrot, onion and garlic to the saucepan and cook over medium-low heat until soft, about 3–4 minutes.

Using a slotted spoon, gently lift out the soaked porcini, disturbing the liquid as little as possible – if any dirt has been dislodged from the mushrooms by the soaking liquid, you want it to fall to the bottom (reserve the liquid for later). Coarsely chop the porcini and add to the pan. Cook for 3 minutes, then add the tomato paste and let it caramelise for 2 minutes. Pour in the wine, stirring to deglaze, then simmer until reduced to a thick paste. Carefully add three-quarters of the mushroom liquid, leaving behind any grit or dirt, then add the stock and herbs, bring to the boil and season with salt.

FOR THE GNOCCHI
1.5 kg (3 lb 5 oz) Sebago or
    Russet Burbank potatoes
300 g (10½ oz) '00' flour
50 g (½ cup) finely
    grated parmesan
2 teaspoons sea salt
20 g (¾ oz) egg yolk (from 1 egg)
pinch of freshly grated nutmeg,
olive oil

TO FINISH
25 g (1 oz) unsalted butter
good pinch of finely chopped
    flat-leaf parsley leaves
35 g (⅓ cup) finely
    grated parmesan
40 g (1½ oz) thinly shaved
    pecorino pepato

Pour the contents of the frying pan over the duck legs, cover really tightly with a lid or foil and cook in the oven for 1½ hours, or until the meat falls off the bone.

Meanwhile, for the gnocchi, wash the potatoes and put them into a pan of cold salted water. Bring to the boil, then simmer until tender (about 40 minutes) and drain. When the potatoes are cool enough to handle, peel off the skins and discard. Pass the peeled potatoes through a drum sieve, cover with a clean tea towel and leave to cool completely.

Weigh out 1 kg (2 lb 4 oz) of the potato and mix with the other gnocchi ingredients until you have a smooth dough. Take care not to overwork. Divide the dough into six balls. Working with one ball at a time, roll on a lightly floured surface to form a log 1.5 cm (⅝ inch) wide, then cut into pieces 1.5 cm (⅝ inch) long. Repeat with the remaining dough.

Cook a third of the gnocchi in plenty of boiling salted water until they rise to the surface, about 2 minutes. Using a slotted spoon, transfer the gnocchi to a bowl of iced water to stop the cooking, then drain and lightly oil them, so they don't stick together. (The rest of the gnocchi – if left uncooked – can be kept in the freezer for up to a month and cooked from frozen.)

Remove the ragu from the oven, uncover, and leave to rest for 15 minutes. Take the duck legs out of the liquid and, when cool enough to handle, pick the meat off the bones in big chunks, discarding the skin, bones and herb stalks. Return the meat to the ragu and stir well.

To finish, put a third of the ragu into a large frying pan and bring to a simmer before stirring through the butter and parsley. (The remaining ragu will last in the fridge for 3–4 days, or in the freezer for at least a month.)

Re-heat the gnocchi in boiling water until they float, then drain and add to the frying pan. Toss them with the ragu for 30 seconds, then add the parmesan and toss for another 30 seconds until the ragu has emulsified.

Serve in warmed bowls, with the thinly shaved pecorino pepato.

Pictured on previous page; gnocchi-making process shown on following pages

PASTA, FILLED AND SHAPED

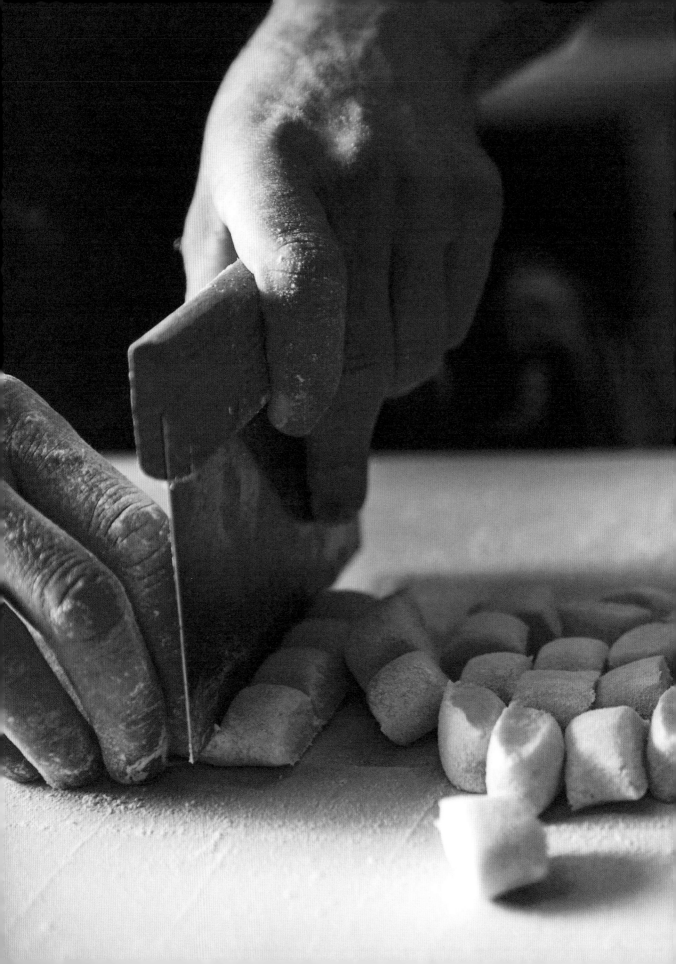

Sorpresine cacio e pepe

Sorpresine is like an open ravioli but easier to make, as there's no filling. You cut your squares of pasta and then fold them as you would for a filled pasta, but they're left open at the sides. It's a cool shape that grabs and holds sauce really well. This cacio e pepe sauce is not done the traditional way, but it is bulletproof and delicious.

SERVES 4

1 quantity master pasta dough
   (see page 23), rolled
   into sheets 1–1.5 mm
   ($1/16$ inch) thick
250 ml (1 cup) chicken stock
75 g (¾ cup) finely grated
   parmesan, plus extra to serve
100 g (1 cup) finely
   grated pecorino
2–3 tablespoons freshly ground
   pepper
sea salt – optional

First shape the pasta. Cut the sheets into 6 cm (2½ inch) squares. Take a square and fold one corner over to the opposite corner to make a triangle, but only press the pasta together where the two corners meet and do not seal the sides, keeping the centre hollow. Next use your thumbs to gently push the middle of the folded edge away from you, at the same time using your fingers to bring the other two corners forward and pinch them together. Repeat until all the pasta is shaped into sorpresine, then leave to dry on a semolina-dusted surface for 1–2 hours.

For the sauce, warm the stock to 60–70°C (140–158°F) – if you don't have a thermometer, you can bring the stock almost to the boil, then remove from the heat and let it cool for a couple of minutes. Pour the stock into a blender, add both cheeses and blend until really well emulsified and creamy.

In the meantime, cook the sorpresine in plenty of boiling salted water until al dente, about 2–3 minutes, depending on how long the pasta has been drying for.

Drain the sorpresine into a large saucepan, retaining just enough of their cooking water to prevent them from sticking. Grind in as much pepper as you can handle – it is one of the main ingredients in cacio e pepe, after all.

Add half of the cheese emulsion and toss the pasta until it starts to get dry. Add the rest of the cheese emulsion, season with salt, if needed, and keep tossing until the sauce has the right consistency – you want it to be thick and creamy.

Serve in warmed bowls, with the extra parmesan (or some more pecorino, if you prefer), and eat immediately.

Sorpresine-making process shown on following pages

96

Casarecce with pork sausage & radicchio

Casarecce is usually a machine-extruded pasta, but you can make a version at home by rolling strips of pasta dough around a 'ferretto' skewer or knitting needle, using the technique described in the fusilli recipe on page 106. Otherwise, just buy the extruded stuff. And if you want to make this dish even easier, get some quality sausages from your butcher, although preparing the sausage meat yourself will always give you a superior result.

SERVES 2

200 g (7 oz) sausage meat (see page 220) or Italian-style pork and fennel sausages, casings removed
2 large cloves of garlic, finely chopped
½ long red chilli, finely chopped
1 teaspoon finely chopped sage leaves
50 ml (1½ fl oz) dry white wine dry white wine
225 g (8 oz) quality dried casarecce
75 g (2½ oz) radicchio (about half a small head), washed and torn into large chunks
2 tablespoons finely grated parmesan
1 tablespoon finely chopped flat-leaf parsley leaves
olive oil
sea salt and freshly ground pepper

To cook the sausage, place a large frying pan over medium-high heat and add 2 tablespoons of olive oil. When the oil is hot, add the sausage meat in large pieces and fry for about 4–5 minutes, or until golden all over.

Reduce the heat to low, add the garlic, chilli and sage and cook for 1–2 minutes, making sure the garlic doesn't get too dark. Pour in the wine, stirring to deglaze the pan, and simmer until it has almost completely evaporated.

In the meantime, cook the casarecce in plenty of boiling salted water until al dente, according to the instructions on the package.

To finish, pour a ladle of the boiling pasta water over the sausage mixture, then add the radicchio and cook for 1 minute, just to soften it a little.

Drain the pasta (reserving some of the pasta water) and add to the sausage mixture and radicchio, along with the parmesan and parsley. Toss everything together thoroughly, then taste for salt, toss again and add some of the reserved pasta water, if needed.

Serve in warmed bowls, with a drizzle of olive oil and a heap of freshly ground pepper.

Cannelloni with smoked eggplant & ricotta

With cannelloni, it is very important to let the pasta dry for several hours at least, but ideally overnight. This enables it to keep its shape and integrity once it's filled. Ricotta salata is simply a version of the classic fresh Italian cheese that has been salted and dried; you should be able to find it in delicatessens and specialist grocers.

SERVES 4

1 quantity master pasta dough (see page 23), rolled into sheets 2–3 mm (⅛ inch) thick
½ quantity Napoli tomato sauce (see page 219)
100 g (1 cup) finely grated parmesan
75 g (2½ oz) finely grated ricotta salata
basil oil (see page 206), or fresh basil leaves

FOR THE FILLING
1 kg (2 lb 4 oz) eggplants (aubergines)
125 g (4½ oz) fresh ricotta
50 g (½ cup) finely grated parmesan
1 egg
finely grated zest of 1 lemon
1 tablespoon olive oil
sea salt and freshly ground pepper

For the cannelloni, lay out the pasta sheets on a lightly floured workbench or wooden board and cut a 9 cm (3½ inch) square, then check that when you roll it around your rolling pin the pasta just overlaps by 3–4 mm (⅛ inch) – you may need to adjust the size of the square, based on the thickness of your rolling pin. Once you get the size right, cut the pasta sheets into squares.

Lightly brush the front edge of a pasta square with water and wrap it around the rolling pin, pressing down firmly where the two edges meet. Gently pull the cannelloni off the rolling pin and place it upright on the work surface so it holds its shape. Repeat until all the cannelloni are made, then leave to dry for several hours, preferably overnight.

For the filling, preheat the barbecue or grill to medium-high. Cook the eggplants whole, turning every 5 minutes, until the skin is burned and the flesh is cooked all the way through – this should take around 30 minutes, depending on their size. When the eggplants are cool enough to handle, scoop out the flesh, discarding the burned skins and stems. Strain off any excess liquid, then transfer 275 g (9¾ oz) eggplant flesh to a mixing bowl and mix well with all the other filling ingredients. (Any remaining eggplant flesh can be seasoned with salt and mixed with a little grated garlic, olive oil and parsley for some really delicious crostini.)

Preheat the oven to 190°C (375°F) fan-forced.

The easiest way to fill the cannelloni is with a piping bag, but you can use a teaspoon. Only fill them about 90 per cent full, or the filling will come out of the pasta in the oven.

Pour two-thirds of the tomato sauce into a baking dish that just holds your filled cannelloni snugly, spreading it out evenly. Place the cannelloni on top, arranging them side by side, then pour the rest of the sauce over. Sprinkle with the parmesan, cover with foil and cook in the oven for 15 minutes. Uncover and continue cooking for another 10–15 minutes until golden brown. Finish with the ricotta salata and a drizzle of basil oil.

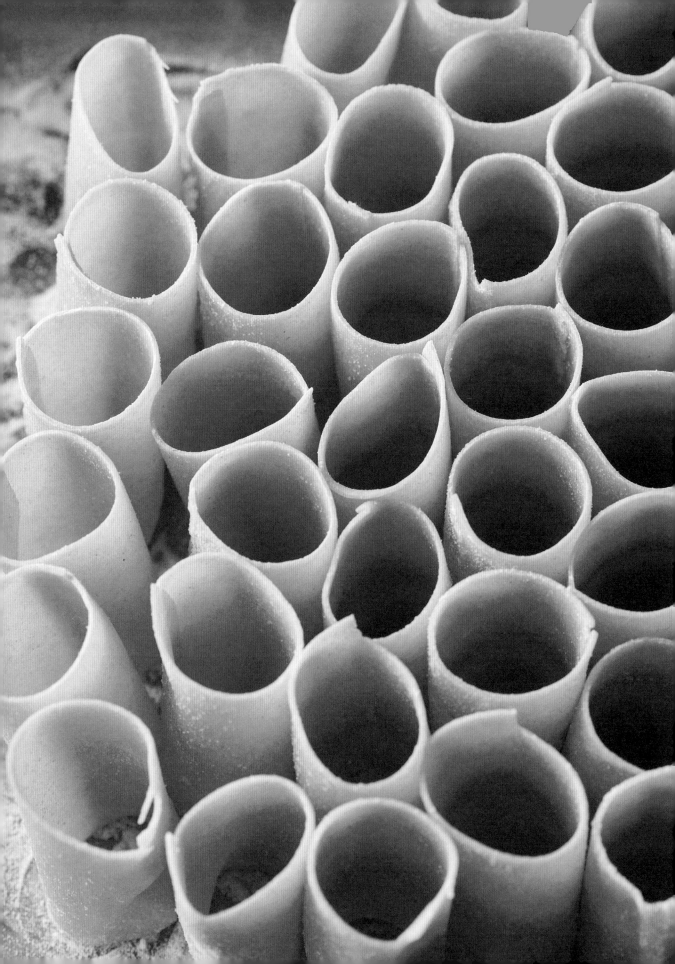

Fusilli al ferretto with puttanesca sauce

Making fusilli is quite easy with a little practice, but it's the kind of pasta you shape one piece at a time, so it's perhaps not the best one to do if you're feeding a crowd. There are a few variants of the 'ferretto' skewer (see page 32) that's traditionally used to shape this pasta: I find the square one to be the most effective, but you can also improvise with a knitting needle or metal skewer – it will just be slightly harder to pull off the finished fusilli. As this is my version of puttanesca, it's a little different. I use heaps of spices and then pass the sauce through a sieve to give it a very fine texture.

SERVES 4

FOR THE PASTA DOUGH
300 g (10½ oz) '00' flour
100 g (3½ oz) wholemeal flour
1 teaspoon sea salt
1 tablespoon olive oil

FOR THE PUTTANESCA SAUCE
1 teaspoon chilli flakes
2 teaspoons fennel seeds
½ teaspoon coriander seeds
100 g (3½ oz) anchovy fillets
   in olive oil
150 ml (5 fl oz) olive oil
2 cloves of garlic, thinly sliced
2 x 400 g (14 oz) tins of peeled
   tomatoes, preferably Italian

At Tipo, we make our fusilli pasta dough in a mixer fitted with the hook attachment by simply mixing all the ingredients with 200 g (7 oz) of water for 5–6 minutes until smooth and elastic.

However, this dough is also easy to mix by hand. In a large bowl, combine both flours and the salt. Make a well in the centre and pour in 200 g (7 oz) of water. With a fork, slowly mix the water with the flour until it has a crumble-like consistency. Add the olive oil, then transfer the dough to a clean work surface and knead with your palms, pushing forward and folding, until the dough is elastic and smooth but not too soft, about 10 minutes.

Wrap the dough really tightly in plastic film or reusable food wrap and set aside at room temperature for at least 30 minutes. I find it better to use this dough on the same day it's made.

To shape the fusilli, on a lightly floured workbench or wooden board, cut off a piece of dough and roll it into a long, skinny log about 5 mm (¼ inch) thick, then cut 4–5 cm (1½–2 inches) long strips off the log. Place your ferretto (or knitting needle or skewer) at a 45-degree angle on one of the long sides of the strip and slowly roll forward, lightly pressing evenly on both sides of the ferretto. When the spiral is complete, gently pull it away from the ferretto and place on a flour-dusted surface. Repeat until all the fusilli are shaped, then leave to dry for 1–2 hours.

For the puttanesca sauce, place a heavy-based saucepan over medium-low heat and toast the chilli flakes, fennel seeds and coriander seeds for 3–4 minutes, watching them carefully as they can quickly burn. Add the anchovies and their oil, together with the olive oil and garlic, and cook over the lowest possible heat until the anchovies break down, then add the tomatoes and cook, still over the lowest possible heat, for 1 hour. Pass the sauce through a fine sieve and discard all the seeds – you should have an intense, oily sauce.

TO FINISH
40 g (1½ oz) capers
60 g (2¼ oz) mixed olive cheeks
4 tablespoons finely
    grated pecorino

Cook the fusilli in plenty of boiling salted water until al dente, about 3–4 minutes, depending on how long the pasta has been drying for.

In the meantime, to finish, place a large frying pan over medium-low heat and warm the capers and olive cheeks for 2–3 minutes. Add the sauce and bring to a simmer.

Drain the pasta and add to the frying pan, then toss thoroughly, making sure the fusilli are well coated with the sauce. Stir in the pecorino and taste for salt.

Serve in warmed bowls.

Pictured overleaf

LUKE'S WINE MATCHES

Italian rosé walks the fine line between a light red and a rosé – but, either way, that is the style of wine to be enjoyed with this pasta! Perhaps something with a volcanic influence, such as a Nerello Mascalese from Mount Etna, or a New World rosé from Mount Macedon, Victoria, where the high altitude ensures textured wines.

Fusilli al ferretto with puttanesca sauce (see previous page)

Pumpkin cappellacci with bergamot

A very traditional recipe (aside from the bergamot) from Ferrara, where Alberto is from. You can use fresh bergamot, though it can be hard to find. We tend to use bergamot essential oil – you need to be careful with it, though, because it's very intense. You don't want too much liquid in the filling, either, so use a firm pumpkin that's not too juicy, like a Japanese pumpkin. When in season, we use locally farmed Galeux d'Eysines pumpkins.

SERVES 4

1 quantity master pasta
    dough (see page 23),
    rolled into sheets 1–1.5 mm
    (1/16 inch) thick
100 g (3½ oz) unsalted butter
1 tablespoon chopped sage
    leaves – optional
2 tablespoons finely
    grated parmesan
olive oil
sea salt and freshly
    ground pepper
a little basil oil or herb oil
    (see page 206) – optional

FOR THE FILLING
2 kg (4 lb 8 oz) pumpkin,
    preferably Japanese
    or Galeux d'Eysines
150 g (5½ oz) shallots,
    thinly sliced
300 g (10½ oz) finely
    grated parmesan
few drops of bergamot
    essential oil
freshly grated nutmeg

For the filling, preheat the oven to 180°C (350°F) fan-forced. Cut the pumpkin in half and scoop out the seeds. Depending on the size of the pumpkin, cut each half into two or three pieces and place on a baking tray. Drizzle lightly with olive oil and season with salt and pepper, then cover with foil and roast for about an hour, or until almost cooked. Uncover and cook for another 15–20 minutes, until the pumpkin is completely cooked and almost dry. When it's cool enough to handle, scoop all the flesh from the skin and set aside – you need 1 kg (2 lb 4 oz) pumpkin flesh for the filling.

In a large heavy-based saucepan, cook the shallot in a little olive oil over low heat until translucent, then add the pumpkin flesh and crush it with a whisk until smooth. Stir in the parmesan and a few drops of bergamot oil, being careful not to overpower the mix, then season to taste with nutmeg, salt and pepper and remove from the heat. Cover the filling with plastic film, pressing it directly onto the surface to prevent a skin forming, then leave in the fridge to cool completely.

In the meantime, for the pasta, lay out the pasta sheets on a lightly floured workbench or wooden board and cut into 8 cm (3¼ inch) squares; if you want your cappellacci to have crinkly edges, use a fluted pastry wheel. Place a heaped tablespoon of the filling in the centre of each square and brush or lightly spray around it with a little water. Fold one corner over to the opposite side to make a triangle and press around the edges to seal the cappellacci, taking care not to trap any air inside. Take the two corners, twist so they meet, and pinch firmly. Repeat until all the filling and pasta is used. Leave the cappellacci to dry for 30 minutes at room temperature, or for up to 24 hours in the fridge, uncovered.

Cook the cappellacci in plenty of boiling salted water for about 4–5 minutes until al dente, depending on how long the pasta has been drying for.

Meanwhile, place a large frying pan over medium-high heat.

When it's hot, add the butter – it should start foaming straight away – and cook until golden brown and starting to smell nutty. Add the sage, if using, and season with salt, then add small ladlefuls of the boiling pasta water, one at a time, and stir until the sauce has emulsified.

When the cappellacci are done, use a slotted spoon to carefully lift them out of the water and transfer them to the frying pan. Gently toss over low heat to make sure the cappellacci are well coated with the sauce. Add the parmesan and taste for salt, then keep tossing until the sauce is thick and smooth.

Serve in warmed bowls, with a few drops of basil or herb oil, if you have some to hand.

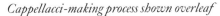

Cappellacci-making process shown overleaf

PASTA, FILLED AND SHAPED

LUKE'S GUIDE
to Pasta & Wine Matching

Pasta and wine, or wine and pasta? They go hand in hand, and I often find myself choosing the bottle of wine first! Hundreds of years of hard work and dedication have gone into getting the balance of flavours right, so it's something of a culinary adventure that everyone should experience to see what works best for them.

In Italy, wine matching is traditionally all about the region, based on the belief that what grows together goes together. There are times of the year when this seasonality is at its peak: the amazing harmony between the truffles of Piedmont and a bottle of barolo, for example; or the incredible, perfectly sweet clams you get in the depths of winter that just cry out for a glass of soave.

For us down here, in the 'region' of Australia – just a little south of Italy – we pay huge respect to these historic pairings and then add a little spin of our own. In the New World, the rules aren't as hard and fast, which allows us to approach things in a less traditional way, which can result in something surprising or unexpected. Pairing a crab pasta with a salty Sicilian white is always a great match, but why not try a richer, broader wine like a rosé? This can add an extra dimension to the dish, bringing chilli and herbal notes to the fore.

The basics of pairing wine with pasta come down to a few key elements – salinity, richness and earthiness. If you focus on these aspects, you could be in for one of those culinary experiences that we search for daily in the restaurant.

SALT/SALINITY
With pasta dishes, when we talk about salinity we're mainly talking about fish and seafood, so focus your wine search on what you would want to accompany that. Look for something with citrus flavours – a wine that's high in acidity and minerality. Think Italian wines from grapes grown on the volcanic soils of Campania or Mount Etna.

RICHNESS
Richness can come from seafood or red meat. The likes of lobster, shellfish and sea urchin are very powerful, densely flavoured ingredients that require a powerful, acid-driven wine for balance. This can come in the form of a wine with a touch of residual sugar, such as chenin blanc or riesling, or a wine high in acid that can handle a little oak, such as chardonnay or verdicchio.

But it is when matching wine with a rich, meaty ragu that you can really bring out the big guns. With Italian wines your best bet is to head straight for nebbiolo and sangiovese grapes, while in the New World you're going to have a good time with wines made from shiraz and cabernet varieties.

EARTHINESS
Some of the best bowls of pasta I've ever had focus on seasonal vegetables, giving them an earthy, vegetal character. Think orecchiette with cime di rapa (see page 146) or a classic trofie with pesto. Here I find lighter red wines with some savoury spice enhance the flavours: something like a New World pinot noir, a nebbiolo from the Roero area of Piedmont or a nerello mascalese from Mount Etna. You could even throw a medium-bodied, maritime-influenced white at them, such as a New World pinot gris or a pigato from Liguria.

Potato & cauliflower tortelloni with sage butter

This is a great winter dish. I like to use Royal Blue potatoes because they are waxy and firm and don't go mushy, so you'll still end up with lots of texture in the filling. If you can't get these, other waxy potatoes such as kipfler, Bintje or Dutch Cream will do the trick.

SERVES 4

1 quantity master pasta dough
   (see page 23), rolled into
   sheets 1–1.5 mm (1/16 inch) thick
sea salt and freshly
   ground pepper

FOR THE FILLING

200 g (7 oz) waxy potatoes,
   ideally Royal Blue, peeled and
   cut into 1 cm (½ inch) cubes
150 g (5½ oz) cauliflower florets,
   coarsely chopped
2–3 tablespoons olive oil
1 tablespoon chopped
   flat-leaf parsley leaves
1 small clove of garlic,
   finely chopped
40 g (1½ oz) unsalted butter
1 large shallot, finely diced
40 g (1½ oz) plain
   (all-purpose) flour
300 ml (10½ fl oz) whole milk,
   warmed
50 g (½ cup) finely
   grated parmesan

For the filling, boil the potatoes in salted water for 2–3 minutes until just cooked. Drain and set aside.

Place a large frying pan over high heat and saute the cauliflower in the olive oil for 2 minutes. Reduce the heat to low, add the parsley and garlic and season with a little salt. Cook for another minute, then set aside with the potatoes.

Melt the butter in a heavy-based saucepan and cook the shallot until translucent. Add the flour and cook for 3–4 minutes over low heat, stirring with a wooden spoon. Gradually whisk in the warm milk until smooth, then cook for 10 minutes over the lowest possible heat to thicken, stirring to avoid it catching on the bottom. Add the potatoes and cauliflower to the sauce and cook for 5 more minutes, to the point where the potatoes are starting to break down without collapsing completely into mash. Stir in the parmesan and season with salt and pepper.

Transfer the filling to a baking tray or dish and cover with plastic film, pressing it directly onto the surface to prevent a skin forming, then leave in the fridge to cool completely.

To shape the tortelloni, place the pasta sheets on a lightly floured workbench or wooden board. Using a 9 cm (3½ inch) round pastry cutter, cut as many circles as possible out of each sheet.

Place a tablespoon of the filling in the centre of each circle and brush or lightly spray around it with a little water. Fold one side over to the other to make a semicircle and press around the edges to seal the ravioli, taking care not to trap any air inside. Take the two corners, twist until they meet and pinch together firmly – you need to press the join enough to make the pasta the same thickness all around the tortelloni. Repeat until all the filling and pasta is used, then leave the tortelloni to dry for 30 minutes at room temperature, or for up to 24 hours in the fridge, uncovered.

Cook the tortelloni in plenty of boiling salted water until al dente, 4–6 minutes, depending on how long the pasta has been drying for.

TO FINISH

75 g (2½ oz) unsalted butter
100 g (3½ oz) cauliflower
    florets, broken into 1 cm
    (½ inch) pieces
1 tablespoon small sage leaves
50 g (½ cup) finely
    grated parmesan

In the meantime, to finish, place a large frying pan over medium-high heat and add the butter. Brown the butter until it smells nutty, being careful not to let it burn. Reduce the heat to low, add the cauliflower florets and sage, then season with salt and cook for 2–3 minutes, or until the cauliflower is tender. Add a ladle of the boiling pasta water to the frying pan and toss to emulsify.

When the tortelloni are done, use a slotted spoon to carefully lift them out of the water and transfer them to the frying pan. Gently toss over low heat to make sure they are well coated with the sauce. Add the parmesan and toss until well emulsified. If the sauce gets too thick or splits, adjust with some of the pasta water. Serve on warmed plates.

Tortelloni-making process shown on following pages

PASTA, FILLED AND SHAPED

Risotto

Nettle & pink peppercorn risotto

Nettles are at their best in spring. They're considered a weed so you can pick them yourself, if you know what you're looking for, or buy them from a farmers' market. For this dish I don't really like to suggest an alternative to the nettles, as their flavour is intense and very particular; they also give the risotto an amazing bright green colour. Saltbush grows everywhere in Australia. Some markets and greengrocers might have it, but you can also go out and find it growing wild, as long as you're confident of your ability to forage safely and respectfully.

SERVES 4

½ brown onion, finely diced
320 g (11¼ oz) Vialone Nano rice
80 ml (⅓ cup) dry white wine
1 litre (4 cups) vegetable
    or chicken stock
90 g (3¼ oz) cold unsalted
    butter, diced
125 g (4½ oz) finely
    grated parmesan
40 g (1½ oz) saltbush
    or sage leaves
finely grated zest of 1 lemon
2 tablespoons pink peppercorns
sea salt
olive oil

FOR THE NETTLE PUREE

1 shallot, thinly sliced
1 clove of garlic, thinly sliced
50 ml (1½ fl oz) olive oil
1 sprig of thyme
50 ml (1½ fl oz) dry white wine
100 ml (3½ fl oz) chicken
    or vegetable stock
125 g (4½ oz) nettle leaves
    (wear gloves when picking)

For the nettle puree, saute the shallot and garlic in the olive oil until soft, then add the thyme and the wine and simmer until the liquid is reduced by half. Pour in the stock and continue simmering until reduced by half. Remove the thyme stalk and set the reduction aside to cool.

Wearing gloves, wash the nettle leaves thoroughly to make sure there is no sand or soil. Blanch the leaves in a pan of boiling salted water for 2–3 minutes, then cool in iced water. Drain the nettles, squeezing out the excess water, then transfer to a small jug or cup. Pour in the cooled reduction and blend with a stick blender until smooth, then season with salt.

To make the risotto, place a wide pan over medium-low heat and saute the onion in about 2 tablespoons of olive oil until translucent. Add the rice and lightly toast for 2 minutes, then season with a pinch of salt. Pour in the white wine and let it evaporate completely. Continue to cook the rice, adding the stock one ladle at a time and stirring every couple of minutes.

When almost all of the stock has been absorbed, about 15 minutes in, the rice should be 90 per cent cooked. If not, add some more stock or water and cook it for a little longer – you want the rice to have a good bite without being crunchy.

Now add the nettle puree and mix until well combined, then proceed with the 'mantecatura' (to make the risotto creamy), stirring in the cold butter one piece at a time. Once that's done, add the parmesan a handful at a time and keep stirring until the risotto is creamy and smooth. If it seems dry, add a little more stock or water.

In the meantime, blanch the saltbush (if using) in a pan of boiling salted water for 1 minute, then refresh in iced water.

To finish, stir half the saltbush or sage and the lemon zest through the risotto, then taste for seasoning and adjust as needed. Serve in warmed bowls, garnished with the pink peppercorns and the rest of the saltbush or sage and drizzled with olive oil.

Fermented mushroom risotto

Mushroom risotto is a classic dish that you can find all over the place. But this is our version, which takes a little longer to prepare and doesn't actually have pieces of mushroom in it! We make a mushroom stock and then, after we strain out the mushrooms, we ferment them for up to a week. The good thing is that slightly older mushrooms work really well for this, so you can often get them on special at the markets. While the stock itself would make a really delicious risotto, when you add a spoonful of the fermented mushroom paste, along with heaps of butter and cheese, the result is complex, super delicious and full of umami flavour. If local truffles are in season, it's worth shaving some fresh truffle over the finished dish.

SERVES 4

2 large shallots, finely chopped
2 tablespoons olive oil
320 g (11½ oz) Vialone Nano rice
80 ml (⅓ cup) white vermouth, such as Cocci Americano, or white wine
100 g (3½ oz) cold unsalted butter, diced
125 g (4½ oz) finely grated parmesan
sea salt

FOR THE STOCK

500 g (1 lb 2 oz) field mushrooms, coarsely chopped
2 large shallots, coarsely chopped
2 teaspoons thyme leaves
2 litres (8 cups) chicken or vegetable stock

For the stock, lightly sprinkle the mushrooms with salt and leave in a warm place in the kitchen for a few hours, preferably overnight. This draws out the juices from the mushrooms and helps to oxidise them, intensifying their flavour.

Put the mushrooms, shallot and thyme into a stockpot or large saucepan, then pour in the stock. Bring to a simmer and cook over low heat for 1½ hours, then take off the heat, cover and let it rest for 30 minutes. Strain the stock through a colander and squeeze the mushrooms to extract as much liquid as possible – you should have about 1–1.5 litres (4–6 cups). Store your stock in the fridge, where it will last well for up to a week, or freeze for longer storage. Keep the mushrooms aside for fermenting.

To lacto-ferment the mushrooms, you will need to weigh them, then make a brine using 2 per cent of the mushrooms' weight in salt – so, if the mushrooms weigh 300 g (10½ oz), you'll need to dissolve 6 g (⅛ oz) of sea salt in 1 litre (4 cups) of filtered or bottled water. Pack the mushrooms into a sterilised 500 ml (2 cup) jar, then pour in enough of the brine to completely cover the mushrooms. Put the lid on the jar and leave at room temperature, away from sunlight, for 4–7 days, briefly opening the lid each day to allow any gases to escape. (If you have a vacuum sealer, you can use that to ferment the mushrooms instead: just seal the mushrooms in a bag with 2 per cent of their weight in salt – you will see that it's working once the bag starts filling up with air.)

After 4 days, taste a little of the ferment each day to check on its progress, resealing and leaving for longer, if needed. When it has reached the desired strength of flavour, strain off the liquid, transfer the fermented mushrooms to a blender or food processor and pulse to a coarsely chopped paste. (If you're not using it right away, the paste can be kept in the fridge for up to 6 months.)

When you're ready to make the risotto, bring your mushroom stock to the boil and keep warm. Place a wide pan over medium-low heat and saute the shallot in the olive oil until translucent. Add the rice and lightly toast for 2 minutes, then pour in the vermouth or wine and let it evaporate completely. Continue to cook the rice, adding the stock one ladle at a time and stirring every couple of minutes.

When almost all of the stock has been absorbed, about 15 minutes in, the rice should be 90 per cent cooked. If not, add some more stock or water and cook it for a little longer – you want the rice to have a good bite without being crunchy.

Now proceed with the 'mantecatura' (to make the risotto creamy), stirring in the cold butter one piece at a time. Once that's done, stir in 2 tablespoons of your fermented mushroom paste, then add the parmesan a handful at a time and keep stirring until the risotto is creamy and smooth. If it seems dry, add a little more stock or water. Check for seasoning, but you shouldn't need any as the fermented mushrooms are quite salty.

Serve the risotto in warmed shallow bowls.

Wild garlic risotto with crab & preserved lemon

For this risotto we use Carnaroli rice, as we do for most of our seafood risottos at Tipo. Compared to Vialone Nano and Arborio, Carnaroli rice has longer grains that keep their shape very well. I also find it to be starchier, which means it works well for seafood risottos where little, if any, cheese is used. In spring, wild garlic is everywhere around Melbourne, but if you can't find it where you live, you could use garlic chives. Traditionally the crab would go in with the rice, however I prefer to cook it separately in oil with some preserved lemon before serving it – and all its lemony, crabby oil – on top of the risotto.

SERVES 4

1 litre (4 cups) fish stock
½ brown onion, finely diced
2 tablespoons olive oil
320 g (11¼ oz) Carnaroli rice
80 ml (⅓ cup) dry white wine
60 g (2¼ oz) cold unsalted
   butter, diced
60 g (2¼ oz) finely
   grated parmesan
squeeze of lemon juice
sea salt
wild garlic, to garnish – optional

FOR THE WILD GARLIC EMULSION
100 ml (3½ fl oz) dry white wine
4 oysters, freshly shucked,
   retaining their juices
50 g (1¾ oz) unsalted
   butter, diced
30 g (1 oz) baby spinach leaves
50 g (1¾ oz) wild garlic,
   roughly chopped

FOR THE CRAB
80 ml (⅓ cup) olive oil
300 g (10½ oz) raw spanner
   crab meat, or other white
   crab meat (preferably raw)
1 preserved lemon, rind only,
   finely diced
1 clove of garlic, finely chopped

For the wild garlic emulsion, bring the wine to the boil in a small non-aluminium pan and simmer until reduced by two-thirds. Turn the heat down to very low, add the oysters with their juices and poach gently for 1 minute. Remove from the heat and stir in the butter one piece at a time until emulsified.

Blanch the baby spinach in boiling water for 1 minute and refresh in iced water, then drain and squeeze out all the excess water.

Put the butter-oyster emulsion into a small jug with the spinach and wild garlic and blend with a stick bender until smooth.

To make the risotto, bring the stock to the boil, then keep it warm. Place a wide pan over medium-low heat and saute the onion in the olive oil until translucent. Add the rice and lightly toast for 2 minutes, then season with a pinch of salt. Pour in the wine and let it evaporate completely. Continue to cook the rice, adding the stock one ladle at a time and stirring every couple of minutes. When almost all of the stock has been absorbed, about 15 minutes in, the rice should be 90 per cent cooked. If not, add some more stock or water and cook it for a little longer – you want the rice to have a good bite without being crunchy.

Now add the wild garlic emulsion and mix until well combined, then proceed with the 'mantecatura' (to make the risotto creamy), stirring in the cold butter one piece at a time. Once that's done, add the parmesan a handful at a time and keep stirring until the risotto is creamy and smooth. If it seems dry, add a little more stock or water. When it's ready, cover with a clean tea towel and leave to rest while you cook the crab.

For the crab, warm the olive oil in a small saucepan and cook the crab over low heat for 2–3 minutes. Add the preserved lemon and garlic, season with salt and cook for another minute.

Finish the risotto with a squeeze of lemon juice, then serve on warmed plates, topped with the crab and its juices, and garnished with some more wild garlic, if you like.

Lobster risotto with zucchini flowers

With the zucchini flowers and the lobster, this is definitely a very summery dish. It's also a great dish to serve at a Christmas or other celebration lunch, because everybody loves lobster. If you can't stomach dealing with a live lobster, buying a whole cooked lobster will still give you a good result. I love yellow tomatoes. As they're sweeter than red tomatoes, they make an amazing sauce, with a light and bright colour.

SERVES 4

1 live or cooked lobster, about 600–800 g (1 lb 5 oz–1 lb 12 oz)
½ brown onion, finely diced
3 tablespoons olive oil
320 g (11¼ oz) Carnaroli rice
80 ml (⅓ cup) dry white wine
60 g (2¼ oz) cold unsalted butter, diced
60 g (2¼ oz) finely grated parmesan
8 female zucchini (courgette) flowers, with baby zucchini attached
finely grated zest of 1 lemon
squeeze of lemon juice
sea salt

FOR THE YELLOW TOMATO BISQUE

100 g (3½ oz) unsalted butter
1 teaspoon fennel seeds
500 g (1 lb 2 oz) yellow tomatoes, grated on a box grater
1.5 litres (6 cups) fish stock
1 sprig of lemon thyme

If you're using a live lobster, chill it in the freezer for 1 hour to 'put it to sleep'. Meanwhile, bring a large saucepan of well-salted water to the boil.

Take the lobster out of the freezer, lay it on a chopping board and insert a knife between the eyes to kill it, cutting right down through the head. Put the lobster into the boiling water and cook for 7–8 minutes, then take it out and let it cool.

To prepare the lobster, twist and pull the lobster head away from the tail. With kitchen scissors, cut down either side of the belly shell and carefully remove the tail meat from the shell. Keep the lobster meat in the fridge and reserve the shell (including the head) for the bisque.

For the bisque, take the lobster shell and separate the top part of the head from the bottom. Wash off all the impurities under cold water, then use a heavy knife to break the shell into smaller pieces. Melt the butter in a saucepan over low heat and saute the lobster shells and fennel seeds for about 10 minutes. Add the tomatoes, stock and lemon thyme and bring to a simmer, then cover with a lid and cook gently for 45 minutes. Strain the bisque through a colander into a clean container, using the back of a ladle or a big wooden spoon to press down on the shells and extract all the juices. Let it cool for 10 minutes and blend with a stick blender until smooth. Pass through a sieve again, then set aside – you'll need about 1.5 litres (6 cups) of bisque.

To make the risotto, bring 1 litre (4 cups) of the bisque to the boil and keep warm. Place a wide pan over medium-low heat and saute the onion in the olive oil until translucent. Add the rice and lightly toast for 2 minutes, then season with a pinch of salt. Pour in the white wine and let it evaporate completely. Continue to cook the rice, adding the bisque one ladle at a time and stirring every couple of minutes.

When almost all of the bisque has been absorbed, about 15 minutes in, the rice should be 90 per cent cooked. If not, add some more bisque or water and cook it for a little longer – you want the rice to have a good bite without being crunchy.

Now proceed with the 'mantecatura' (to make the risotto creamy), stirring in the cold butter one piece at a time. Once that's done, add the parmesan a handful at a time and keep stirring until the risotto is creamy and smooth. If it seems dry, add a little more stock or water.

Thinly slice the baby zucchini, saving the flowers for garnish, and stir through the risotto, then add the lemon zest and lemon juice and check for seasoning.

Cut the lobster in half lengthwise and remove the dark digestive tract. Cut the lobster meat into large chunks and gently warm in the remaining 500 ml (2 cups) of the bisque, along with the zucchini flowers.

Serve the risotto on warmed plates, topped with the lobster and zucchini flowers.

Pictured overleaf

LUKE'S WINE MATCHES

A decadent seafood risotto with earthy notes calls for an equally powerful wine. Think lean, flinty chardonnay from Chablis, or richer vintages from Puligny Montrachet and Chassagne Montrachet. Of course there are alternatives to burgundy – try whites from the Collio region of north-eastern Italy, bordering Slovenia, or seek out a cool-climate Victorian or Tasmanian chardonnay.

Lobster risotto with zucchini flowers (see previous page)

Home
Classics

Lasagne

We've never had lasagne on the menu at Tipo, but I've made many versions at home over the years. As there are quite a few elements to make, it can be really time consuming and not so much fun to try and do everything from scratch on the day. I always have at least the ragu made in advance, but if the pasta dough is ready to go too, then it streamlines the rest of the process. And if you're really pushed for time, ready-made fresh lasagne sheets from your local deli would also work well.

SERVES 6-8

1 quantity master pasta dough (see page 23)

1 quantity ragu Bolognese (see page 136)

500 ml (2 cups) Napoli tomato sauce (see page 219)

175 g (1¾ cups) finely grated parmesan

FOR THE BECHAMEL SAUCE

100 g (3½ oz) unsalted butter

100 g (3½ oz) plain (all-purpose) flour

750 ml (3 cups) whole milk, warmed

25 g (¼ cup) finely grated parmesan

sea salt and freshly ground pepper

freshly grated nutmeg

Roll the pasta dough (see page 24) into sheets 2–3 mm (⅛ inch) thick and about 10–12 cm (4–4½ inches) wide, roughly the width of the rollers in most pasta machines. You should be able to get 8–10 sheets, which will give you a lasagne of 4–5 layers. Lightly dust the pasta sheets with semolina flour and set aside.

For the bechamel sauce, melt the butter in a small saucepan over low heat. Add the flour and cook for 3–4 minutes, stirring with a wooden spoon. Gradually whisk in the warm milk until smooth, then cook for 10 minutes over the lowest possible heat to thicken, stirring to avoid the sauce catching on the bottom. Remove from the heat, stir in the parmesan and season with salt, pepper and a hint of nutmeg.

If you made the ragu Bolognese ahead of time, put it into a saucepan and bring it to a simmer; you may need to add a little water or stock to loosen it up. Do the same with the tomato sauce.

When you have all your components ready to go, preheat the oven to 175°C (350°F) fan-forced.

To assemble your lasagne, choose a baking dish about 35 × 24 cm (14 × 9½ inches). Set aside roughly a third of the parmesan for the top, then start building the layers. Spread 3–4 spoons of the ragu over the bottom of your baking dish, followed by a couple of spoons of the tomato sauce, just so the pasta sheets don't stick. Lay in two sheets of pasta side by side and randomly spoon dollops of the bechamel over the top, then spoon over another layer of ragu and tomato sauce and sprinkle with some parmesan. Continue this layering process until all the pasta, ragu and tomato sauce is used, then finish with the reserved parmesan.

Cook the lasagne, uncovered, for 50 minutes–1 hour. Check on it after 45 minutes: if the top is getting too dark, reduce the oven temperature to 150°C (300°F); if it looks too pale, increase the temperature to 200°C (400°F) for the remaining cooking time.

Once it's ready, let it rest for an hour before cutting and serving.

Garganelli with ragu Bolognese

As with most recipes, the secret here lies in the quality of the ingredients. I choose the meat for this ragu with the same level of scrutiny and care as I do when choosing a steak. With ready-minced meat, the flavour will vary, and if the fat content is too low it can be very dry by the time you've cooked your ragu. By mincing it myself, I can regulate both the cut of meat and the texture of the mince. At home, I use the coarse metal plate of the food grinder attachment on my KitchenAid mixer. It takes a few minutes and is time well spent, but if you can't or don't want to do the mincing yourself, just order the same cuts from your butcher and ask them to coarsely mince the meat for you.

The ragu makes more than you need for two people – in fact, it will serve six generously – but the rest will last in the fridge for 3–4 days, or in the freezer for at least a month. If, on the other hand, you're cooking for more than two, you could increase the quantity of pasta accordingly and then complete the dish in several pans, unless you have a really large pan that will comfortably fit the amount of pasta and sauce so they can be tossed and emulsified properly.

Traditionally garganelli is shaped using a 'pettine' pasta comb and a pencil-like wooden stick. I use a ribbed gnocchi board, along with a dowel about 5 mm (¼ inch) in diameter that was part of a set of rolling pins for pasta making (see page 32).

SERVES 2

½ quantity master pasta dough (see page 23), rolled into sheets 2–3 mm (⅛ inch) thick
olive oil
cracked black pepper
finely grated parmesan, to serve

To shape the garganelli, lay out the pasta sheets on a lightly floured bench and cut into 4 cm (1½ inch) squares. Place a pasta square on the ribbed wooden board, then wrap the pasta around the dowel diagonally as you roll it across the board, pressing firmly at the join. Pull the pasta off the dowel and set aside on a semolina-dusted surface. Repeat until all the garganelli are made, then leave to dry for 3–4 hours.

In the meantime, make the ragu Bolognese. Place a large heavy-based saucepan over medium-high heat, add the olive oil and both meats and brown for about 5 minutes, or until it starts caramelising, breaking it up as it cooks – a whisk is good for this. If your pan isn't big enough to hold it all comfortably, do this in two batches. Remove the meat with a slotted spoon, so the rendered fat stays in the pan, and set aside.

Reduce the heat to medium-low, add the onion, carrot, celery and garlic to the pan and cook slowly until soft, at least 5 minutes – you may need to add a little more oil, depending on how much fat has rendered from the meat. Return the meat to the pan, stir in the tomato paste and cook for 2–3 minutes, then pour in the wine, stirring to deglaze, and simmer until almost completely evaporated.

FOR THE RAGU BOLOGNESE
about 125 ml (½ cup) olive oil
500 g (1 lb 2 oz) beef neck
    or chuck, coarsely minced
300 g (10½ oz) pork scotch
    or shoulder, coarsely minced
1 brown onion, diced
1 carrot, diced
1 small celery stalk, diced
2 cloves of garlic, finely chopped
125 g (4½ oz) tomato paste
    (concentrated puree)
250 ml (1 cup) red wine
2 cloves
2 sprigs of thyme
1 bay leaf
400 ml (14 fl oz) chicken stock,
    plus extra if needed
sea salt and freshly
    ground pepper

Wrap the cloves, thyme and bay leaf in a piece of muslin (cheesecloth) and tie with string. Add this to the pan and pour in the stock, then season with salt and pepper. Cover with a lid and let the ragu simmer over low heat for 45 minutes–1 hour, stirring occasionally and adding more stock if it gets too dry.

Cook the garganelli in plenty of boiling salted water until al dente, about 3–4 minutes, depending on how long the pasta has been drying for.

Meanwhile, spoon a third of the ragu into a large frying pan and bring to a simmer.

Drain the pasta and add it to the frying pan, then toss until it is well coated with the ragu.

Serve in warmed bowls, with a generous amount of olive oil, cracked black pepper and parmesan.

Pictured overleaf; garganelli-making process shown on following pages

LUKE'S WINE MATCHES

This dish just screams out for a generously fruited red with notes of spice and earth. I'm a big fan of a warm-climate sangiovese to go with a classic ragu Bolognese, my first choice being a Rosso di Montepulciano.

Garganelli with ragu Bolognese (see previous page)

Spaghetti carbonara

Try to get a good piece of guanciale (cured pig's cheek) from a deli or speciality butcher – I look for a good amount of fat, as it crisps up really well. I like to make my carbonara with a stock enriched with the guanciale skin and parmesan rinds that would otherwise go into the bin. This adds flavour and gives the carbonara a thick sauce-like texture, rather than the usual gluggy, paste-like one. And as you can almost boil this mixture without it splitting, you don't need to worry so much about scrambling the egg.

SERVES 2

75 g (2½ oz) guanciale
about 500 ml (2 cups) chicken stock
parmesan rinds, if you have any saved up
2 egg yolks
3 tablespoons finely grated pecorino (pepato or romano), plus extra to serve
225 g (8 oz) quality dried spaghetti
freshly ground pepper

Remove the skin from the guanciale (reserving it for the stock), then cut the guanciale into 5 mm (¼ inch) dice.

Bring 400 ml (14 fl oz) of the chicken stock to the boil and add the reserved guanciale skin, along with any parmesan rinds you may have, then simmer gently for 30 minutes. You don't want the stock to reduce too much, so cook it over very low heat. You should end up with about 250 ml (1 cup) – make up this amount with more stock, if needed.

Put the diced guanciale into a frying pan over very low heat and cook slowly until all the fat is rendered and it becomes very crispy – this could take up to 15 minutes.

In the meantime, use a whisk or stick blender to mix the egg yolks and pecorino into the warm stock mixture until emulsified.

Once the guanciale is done, use a slotted spoon to remove the crisp guanciale and set aside. Strain the rendered fat into the egg yolk mixture and whisk or blend again, then pour back into the frying pan and keep warm.

Cook the spaghetti in plenty of boiling salted water until al dente, according to the instructions on the package.

Drain the pasta and add to the frying pan, then toss until the sauce thickens and coats the pasta. Grind in a generous amount of pepper, add the crisp guanciale and toss another couple of times – you may need to adjust the consistency with a little more stock.

Divide between warmed bowls and serve with more grated pecorino.

Orecchiette with cime di rapa, anchovy & pangrattato

Making the orecchiette is time consuming but also fun and rewarding once you get the hang of it. I would recommend making just enough for one or two servings to start with, and don't worry if they don't look perfect. I like to use some rye flour in the dough because it's more textural and more rustic, which suits the traditional nature of this dish. And if you don't have time to make your own orecchiette, you can of course use 225 g (8 oz) of dried orecchiette instead. Although this sauce is simple, it is full of flavour – we always use cime de rapa (also known as broccoli rabe or turnip tops) when it's in season, but at other times of year, try broccolini instead.

SERVES 2

100 g (3½ oz) cime di rapa
  (about half a bunch),
  washed and drained really well
1 clove of garlic, finely chopped
½ long red chilli, finely chopped
4 anchovy fillets in olive oil
  (ideally Sicilian), drained
60 ml (¼ cup) olive oil
finely grated zest of 1 small lemon
1 tablespoon finely chopped
  flat-leaf parsley leaves
2 tablespoons finely
  grated parmesan
pangrattato (see page 211),
  to serve

FOR THE PASTA DOUGH
100 g (3½ oz) light rye flour
40 g (1½ oz) durum wheat
  semolina flour
240 ml (8½ fl oz) water, heated
  to 80°C (176°F)

To make the pasta dough in an electric mixer, simply put all the ingredients into the bowl and mix with the hook attachment for 5–6 minutes until smooth and elastic.

Alternatively, you can mix this dough by hand, as it is easier to work than an egg pasta dough. In a large bowl, mix both flours together, then make a well in the centre and pour in the hot water. With a fork, slowly mix the water with the flours until it has a crumble-like consistency. Transfer to a clean work surface and knead with your palms, pushing forward and folding, until the dough is elastic and smooth but not too soft, about 10 minutes.

Tightly wrap the dough in plastic film or reusable food wrap and leave to rest for at least 30 minutes. I find this dough is best used on the same day it's made.

To shape the orecchiette, cut off a small piece of dough – about 50 g (1¾ oz) is a good size – and roll it into a log around 1 cm (½ inch) wide, then cut off 1 cm (½ inch) nuggets. On a lightly floured bench, use a dinner knife to press down on each nugget of dough, pushing away from you and keeping the pressure consistent – the dough should wrap around the knife. Gently ease the dough off the knife, pushing your thumb inside and turning the orecchiette inside out, then set aside on a semolina-dusted surface. Repeat until all the orecchiette are made, then leave to dry while you start the sauce.

To prepare the cime di rapa, trim off and discard the woody ends, then thinly slice the stalks. Keep the leaves and florets in fairly large chunks.

Place a large frying pan over medium-low heat and slowly cook the garlic, chilli and anchovies in the olive oil for 1–2 minutes. Add the cime di rapa and cook for 2–3 more minutes, or until just tender, then remove from the heat and add a splash of water to stop the cooking and avoid burning the garlic, chilli and anchovies.

Cook the orecchiette in plenty of boiling salted water until al dente, 4–5 minutes, depending on how long the pasta has been drying for.

Drain the pasta (reserving some of the pasta water) and add to the frying pan, along with the lemon zest, parsley and parmesan. Toss everything together over low heat until the oil and parmesan have emulsified, adding a little of the reserved pasta water to bring the sauce together, if needed.

Serve in warmed bowls, with a good amount of pangrattato on top.

Orecchiette-making process shown on following pages

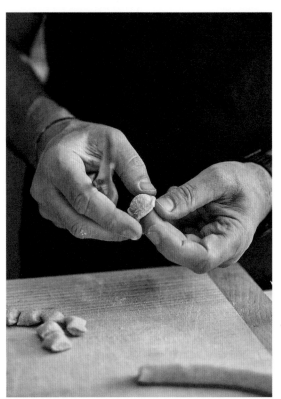

Rigatoni pomodoro

This is a quick and light dish that has become my go-to when hungover, as it's so easily pulled together, especially if you have a batch of Napoli tomato sauce in the freezer and some dried rigatoni in the cupboard. It's also something the kids are always happy to eat.

If you feel like making your own rigatoni, follow the same method as for the garganelli on page 136, but cut the pasta into 4 cm x 3 cm (1½ inch x 1¼ inch) rectangles and roll each one across your ribbed wooden board, aligning the longer sides with the grooves and wrapping the pasta around your wooden dowel to form a tube.

SERVES 2

5 tablespoons olive oil,
   plus extra to serve
1 small clove of garlic,
   finely grated
200 ml (7 fl oz) Napoli tomato
   sauce (see page 219)
225 g (8 oz) quality dried rigatoni
2 tablespoons finely
   grated parmesan
4–5 basil leaves

Warm the olive oil in a pan over medium-low heat, add the garlic and cook gently until the garlic has just softened but not coloured. Add the tomato sauce and bring to a slow simmer.

In the meantime, cook the rigatoni in plenty of boiling salted water until al dente, according to the instructions on the package.

Drain the pasta (reserving some of the pasta water) and add to the sauce, then toss everything together for 30 seconds until the pasta is well coated. Add the parmesan and basil and toss a couple more times, adding a little of the reserved pasta water to adjust the consistency of the sauce, if needed.

Serve in warmed bowls and finish with a drizzle of olive oil.

Spaghetti aglio, olio e peperoncino

I feel like every family in Italy must eat this, or a variation of it, a couple of times per week for lunch. Although it's incredibly tasty, it really doesn't get any easier than this. The only thing to remember is that the garlic needs to be finely grated (or very finely chopped) and cooked slowly, so the dish doesn't taste of raw garlic.

SERVES 2

225 g (8 oz) quality
   dried spaghetti
100 ml (3½ fl oz) olive oil
2 cloves of garlic, finely grated
1 long red chilli, finely chopped
3 tablespoons finely
   chopped flat-leaf
   parsley leaves
2 tablespoons finely grated
   parmesan
sea salt

Cook the spaghetti in plenty of boiling salted water until al dente, according to the instructions on the package.

Meanwhile, warm the olive oil in a frying pan over low heat and gently cook the garlic and chilli until the garlic is translucent. When the garlic and chilli are at the perfect point, stop them cooking any further by removing the pan from the heat and adding a splash of the boiling pasta water. Set aside until the pasta is ready.

Drain the pasta (reserving some of the pasta water) and add to the frying pan, then toss over low heat until it is coated really well, adding enough of the pasta water to loosen the sauce. Sprinkle in the parsley and parmesan, season with salt and keep tossing until well emulsified – the sauce should be thick and oily, and flecked with garlic, chilli and parsley.

Serve in warmed bowls.

MIDNIGHT SPAGHETTI
(Why there is *no excuse* to eat bad food)

Even with the simplest pasta dish, a little extra care and consideration can turn an average meal into an amazing one. This is particularly applicable when you've come home after a night out with friends or working a late shift and you suddenly realise you're famished. Many will opt for the burger/kebab option but, while there's no judgement here, my way of tackling late-night hunger has always been: I'm going home to cook pasta. It doesn't need to be this elaborate thing that'll blow your socks off – just something quick, easy and delicious. This is where midnight spaghetti comes in.

I have a couple of versions of midnight spaghetti that I make depending on my mood and the ingredients I have available. With timing an obvious factor, I always use dried spaghetti, the quality stuff that takes about 15 minutes to cook.

One version is about quickly sauteing garlic, chilli and anchovies, then stirring the cooked pasta through (with some grated bottarga if you have some on hand and want to have a really good time).

The second, even quicker, one is just butter, cheese and black pepper stirred through spaghetti.

It's amazing how delicious midnight spaghetti is. The depth of flavour you can get from just a few ingredients that take only a matter of minutes to prepare is amazing. It's a great one to have in your repertoire, not least because it means never having to eat bad food again.

Not Pasta

Tomato salad with stracciatella & sourdough

For all my tomato salads, I grate some of the tomatoes on a box grater and mix them with the dressing. The technique is based on a Cretan salad called 'dakos', but this is a more Italian version made with sourdough bread, rather than the rye rusks traditionally used in Crete. Only make this dish when you have access to the freshest, ripest tomatoes, otherwise its simplicity and pure flavour will be lost.

SERVES 4

600 g (1 lb 5 oz) mixed heirloom tomatoes
100 ml (3½ fl oz) olive oil, plus extra for drizzling
2 thick slices of sourdough bread, torn into 2–3 cm (1 inch) chunks
75 g (2½ oz) stracciatella, or other fresh curd
sea salt and freshly ground pepper

Preheat the oven to 150°C (300°F) fan-forced.

For the dressing, take about 100 g (3½ oz) of the darker and riper tomatoes and cut them in half. Set your box grater over a mixing bowl and grate the tomato flesh directly into the bowl, discarding the skins. Add half the olive oil and season with salt, then mix with a fork. Set aside.

Tear the bread into 2–3 cm (1 inch) chunks, drizzle with the extra olive oil and season lightly with pepper. Cook in the oven for 10–12 minutes, or until the croutons are crispy on the outside but still chewy on the inside, then allow to cool.

Cut the rest of the tomatoes into large chunks, season well with salt and gently toss with the rest of the olive oil and the sourdough croutons.

Serve the salad with the stracciatella and the dressing spooned over the top.

Asparagus with parmesan mousse & watercress

At Tipo, we usually offer this as an antipasto or a side dish. The hero here is the asparagus, which is lightly chargrilled on the barbecue, but the super-delicious parmesan mousse gets a lot of attention too; the black garlic adds an extra layer of flavour to the mousse, but it's not essential. And for a simpler and lighter dish, you could skip the egg yolk puree.

SERVES 4

1 small bunch of watercress,
    about 75 g (2½ oz)
1 large bunch of asparagus,
    about 16 spears,
    woody ends removed
olive oil
sea salt

FOR THE MOUSSE
1 gold-strength gelatine leaf
125 ml (½ cup) whole milk
70 g (2½ oz) finely
    grated parmesan
20 g (¾ oz) black garlic – optional

FOR THE EGG YOLK PUREE - OPTIONAL
75 g (2½ oz) egg yolk
    (from about 4–5 eggs)
1 teaspoon white wine vinegar
1 teaspoon liquid glucose

For the mousse, soak the gelatine in cold water for 15 minutes. In a small saucepan, gently heat the milk to just below simmering point, 90°C (194°F), then add the squeezed-out gelatine leaf and stir to dissolve completely. Take off the heat and add the parmesan a spoonful at a time, using a stick blender to emulsify. Once all the parmesan is incorporated, add the black garlic (if using) and keep blending until smooth, then pass through a fine sieve into a bowl. Cover with plastic film or reusable food wrap and chill in the fridge until set – at least 3–4 hours, but preferably overnight.

If you're making the egg yolk puree, whisk the egg yolk with the vinegar and glucose in a heatproof bowl. Set the bowl over a pan of gently simmering water (make sure the base of the bowl doesn't touch the water) and slowly bring the egg yolk mixture up to 68–70°C (154–158°F), whisking constantly – this should take about 8–10 minutes. Pass through a fine sieve into a clean container, season with salt and chill in the fridge until needed.

Coarsely chop the watercress, then use a stick blender to blitz to a puree, adding a tablespoon of olive oil and a pinch of salt. Keep blending for about 2 minutes, then pass through a fine sieve, pressing down with the back of a spoon to extract as much juice as possible. Keep in the fridge until needed.

To cook the asparagus, heat a barbecue or griddle pan to medium-high and lightly season the asparagus spears with salt and drizzle with olive oil. Cook the asparagus for about 1 minute on each side, depending on the thickness – you want the asparagus to be pretty tender, warm all the way through and with a little char from the grill.

To serve, arrange the asparagus spears in a row, placing them about 1 cm (½ inch) apart, then spoon or pipe some mousse and egg yolk puree (if using) in the gaps – you want to be more generous with the mousse than with the rich egg yolk puree. Finish with the watercress juice and a little olive oil.

Stuffed sardines

I created this as an antipasto, but when you get really good sardines there's no reason not to serve this as a main dish. Buy the biggest and freshest sardines you can find and, ideally, buy them whole rather than butterflied. They're very easy to clean: you can do it with your hands by just pulling off the head and then running your finger along the length of the sardine to get rid of the guts – you can use a spoon instead of your finger, if you like. Or, if you're a regular customer and know your fishmonger well, you could ask if they'll do the dirty work for you. You want to remove the spine for this recipe too. Again, this is done easily enough with your fingers, but try to keep the two fillets together. Don't go too crazy trying to de-scale them; once you've cooked the sardines in the oven, the scales are fine to eat. If you have any of the blended tomato paste left over, it will last in the fridge for up to a week and you can use it in a Bolognese or any other tomato-based ragu.

SERVES 4

8–12 large sardines, about 600 g (1 lb 5 oz) in total, butterflied (you can ask your fishmonger to do this for you)

FOR THE TOMATO OIL & PASTE
2 small shallots, thinly sliced
2 cloves of garlic, thinly sliced
170 ml (⅔ cup) vegetable oil
125 g (4½ oz) tomato paste (concentrated puree)
1 heaped tablespoon dried oregano

FOR THE STUFFING
100 g (3½ oz) pitted kalamata olives
1 tablespoon finely chopped flat-leaf parsley leaves
1 tablespoon olive oil
1 small clove of garlic, finely grated
50 g (1¾ oz) panko breadcrumbs

For the tomato oil and paste, place a small saucepan over low heat and saute the shallot and garlic in 70 ml (2¼ fl oz) of the vegetable oil. When they are soft and translucent, add the tomato paste and cook for 2–3 minutes, then add the remaining oil and the oregano. Cook over the lowest possible heat for 45 minutes, stirring occasionally so it doesn't catch on the bottom. When it's ready, the oil should be really red and fragrant. Pass it through a sieve lined with a coffee filter, then scrape the paste that's left on the filter into a blender and blend until smooth. If you are using them on the same day, keep the oil and paste at room temperature; otherwise, they can be refrigerated for at least 2 weeks.

When you're ready to cook the sardines, preheat the oven to 200°C (400°F) fan-forced.

For the stuffing, blend all the ingredients except the breadcrumbs in a blender until smooth, then transfer to a bowl and gently mix in the breadcrumbs.

Spoon 2 teaspoons of the stuffing into each sardine, then lay them on a baking tray lined with baking paper. Drizzle with the olive oil and bake for 4–5 minutes, depending on size, then leave to rest for a couple of minutes. Be careful not to overcook the sardines – it is better to cook them to medium, as they'll continue to cook as they rest.

To serve, swirl some of the blended tomato paste across each plate then flood with tomato oil. Divide the sardines between the plates.

Globe artichokes with almond puree & pangrattato

This is one of my favourite dishes. It looks beautiful and is equally lovely to eat, well worth the work involved in preparing fresh artichokes. If you make this when artichokes are at the peak of their season, they will be very tender and easier to clean.

SERVES 4

1 lemon, halved
4 large globe artichokes
½ brown onion, finely diced
40 g (1½ oz) unsalted butter
2 sprigs of thyme
sea salt
pangrattato (see page 211),
　to serve

FOR THE ALMOND PUREE
40 g (1½ oz) stale sourdough
　bread, crusts removed
50 ml (1½ fl oz) olive oil
50 g (1¾ oz) almond meal
1 small clove of garlic,
　finely grated
1–2 tablespoons lemon juice

For the almond puree, soak the sourdough in cold water for about 15 minutes, or until completely soft. Squeeze out most of the water, but keep the bread pretty moist and reserve the squeezed-out water as well. Put the soaked bread into a food processor, add the olive oil, almond meal and garlic and blitz to a mayonnaise consistency – you may need to use some of the reserved water. Add lemon juice and salt to taste. I like the lemon to be quite prominent.

Fill a bowl with cold water, squeeze in the juice of one of the lemon halves and then toss in the squeezed lemon half.

To prepare the artichokes, pull off the first two layers of leaves and discard them, then use a large, serrated knife to cut about a third off the top of the artichoke. Next cut the stem down to about 4 cm (1½ inches) long and, with a peeler, trim away the fibrous part of the stem and all around the artichoke until you see light green/yellow colour and it doesn't feel woody anymore. As a test, pull off a couple of the remaining outer leaves and taste them: they should be almost good enough to eat raw. Now cut the artichoke in half and scoop out the fuzzy and spiky inner choke, if there is any. Immediately put the prepared artichokes into the lemon water to avoid discolouration.

Cook the onion in a saucepan with half the butter for 3–4 minutes until soft and translucent. Add the artichokes and thyme, then pour in enough water to just cover. Season with salt, cover with a lid and simmer for 15–20 minutes, or until the artichokes are tender – a small knife should go through them without much resistance.

Remove the artichokes and keep warm, then add the remaining butter and the juice of the other lemon half and simmer for 3–4 minutes, or until the cooking liquid has reduced to a sauce consistency.

To serve, spoon the almond puree onto each plate and arrange the artichokes over the top. Drench with the sauce, then finish with a generous amount of pangrattato.

Vitello 'anquillato' with capers & parsley

This is my take on vitello tonnato, using smoked eel instead of tuna. You should be able to source smoked eel from most good markets or online. Being hot-smoked, the eel is already cooked, so it's easy to remove the skin and bones – as with smoked trout, you can just pull the flesh from the bones with your fingers (or you could buy smoked eel fillets to make it even easier). For the poached veal I use girello, which is a lean cut from the back leg.

SERVES 4

300 g (10½ oz) veal girello
olive oil
sea salt and freshly
  ground pepper

FOR THE SMOKED EEL MAYONNAISE
125 g (4½ oz) thinly sliced
  shallots (about 3–4 shallots)
100 g (3½ oz) smoked eel flesh
50 g (1¾ oz) dried yellow
  split peas
50 g (1¾ oz) capers
125 ml (½ cup) dry white wine
juice of 1 lemon
100 g (3½ oz) mayonnaise
  (see page 210)

TO FINISH
2 tablespoons capers
1 shallot, thinly sliced
10 g (¼ oz) flat-leaf
  parsley leaves
cracked black pepper

For the smoked eel mayonnaise, saute the shallot in a small saucepan with a little olive oil until translucent. Add the smoked eel, split peas, capers and white wine and cook gently until most of the wine has evaporated.

Pour in 125 ml (½ cup) of water, cover with a lid and simmer until the split peas are soft, about 1 hour. Give it a stir every now and then so it doesn't catch on the bottom, and if it gets too dry, just add a little more water.

Once the split peas are cooked, transfer the contents of the pan to a food processor while still warm and blend to a smooth puree. Squeeze in the lemon juice and season with salt and olive oil. Put in the fridge to cool completely, then fold in the mayonnaise and chill until needed.

To prepare and cook the veal, season it well with salt and pepper, then wrap the meat really tightly in several layers of plastic film, shaping it into a thick sausage and securely tying each end in a knot or with string. Bring a saucepan of water to the boil, then drop in the wrapped veal and simmer for 5 minutes. Turn the heat off, cover the pan with a lid and leave the veal to gently cook in the residual heat for 1 hour.

Take the meat out of the water, remove the plastic film and pat dry with paper towel. Place a frying pan over medium-high heat, add some olive oil and sear the veal for a couple of minutes until nicely browned all over, then remove and leave to cool to room temperature.

To finish, slice the veal across the grain as thinly as possible, then arrange in slightly overlapping layers on a large plate or platter and spoon or pipe small dots of the smoked eel mayonnaise on top of the meat. Garnish with the capers, shallot and parsley and season with cracked pepper.

Stracciatella with pickled raisins, radicchio & saffron

This refined stracciatella dish has sweet, sour, salty and bitter elements, and it works equally well as an antipasto or a standalone salad. The sweet muscatels are briefly pickled before being mingled with a sour and salty dressing, and the shredded radicchio adds crunchy bitterness. I also like to include some chewy sorghum for texture.

SERVES 4

50 g (1¾ oz) sorghum – optional
200 g (7 oz) stracciatella
½ head of radicchio, really
   thinly sliced
sea salt

FOR THE PICKLED RAISINS

75 g (2½ oz) raisins
25 ml (¾ fl oz) white wine vinegar
1 tablespoon caster
   (superfine) sugar

FOR THE SAFFRON DRESSING

0.25 g (¾ teaspoon)
   saffron threads
80 ml (⅓ cup) white wine vinegar
50 ml (1½ fl oz) vegetable oil
50 ml (1½ fl oz) olive oil

For the pickled raisins, put the raisins into a heatproof bowl. In a small non-aluminium pan, bring the vinegar, sugar and 50 ml (1½ fl oz) of water to the boil, then pour it over the raisins and let them soak, covered, for about an hour. Transfer the raisins, with their soaking liquid, to a food processor and blend into a puree.

For the saffron dressing, put the saffron and vinegar into a small non-aluminium pan with 125 ml (½ cup) of water and a pinch of salt. Bring to the boil, then simmer until reduced by two-thirds – you should be left with about 2½ tablespoons. Let the saffron reduction cool to room temperature, then slowly drizzle in the oils, while blending with a stick blender or hand whisk to emulsify.

If using sorghum, cook it in a pan of lightly boiling salted water until tender, about an hour, then drain well.

To serve, put the stracciatella into a bowl and generously dress with most of the saffron dressing, then spoon the raisins and sorghum over the top. Dress the radicchio with the remaining saffron dressing and a pinch of salt, then use to cover the stracciatella.

Chargrilled broccolini with bagna cauda & almonds

This is a simple and really delicious side dish of broccolini bathed in a bagna cauda sauce. In Piedmont, bagna cauda is traditionally made with a lot of anchovies. I make a vegetarian version with almonds, but if you're really into anchovies, feel free to add 40 g (1½ oz) to the sauce halfway through the cooking. Also, it is best to use local organic garlic.

SERVES 4

about 3 heads of garlic, cloves
    separated and peeled –
    you need 125 g (4½ oz)
    peeled garlic
100 ml (3½ fl oz) verjus
75 ml (2½ fl oz) olive oil
75 g (2½ oz) roasted almonds,
    finely chopped
350 g (12 oz) broccolini,
    woody ends of stems removed
sea salt

For the bagna cauda sauce, finely chop the garlic, then blanch it in boiling water for 30 seconds. Drain the garlic in a fine sieve and running it under cold water to cool it down.

Transfer the garlic to a small, heavy-based pan. Add the verjus, olive oil and two-thirds of the almonds and cook over the lowest possible heat, stirring occasionally, for 45 minutes–1 hour until the verjus has evaporated and the garlic starts getting some colour. Remove the sauce from the heat and season with a good amount of salt, then set aside while you cook the broccolini.

Blanch the broccolini in boiling salted water for 30 seconds, then drain. Heat a barbecue or griddle pan to high and char the broccolini for 1 minute on each side. Put the chargrilled broccolini into a bowl with the bagna cauda sauce and gently toss together. Scatter with the remaining almonds to serve.

Octopus with leek & salsa verde

I love chargrilled octopus. I must have done about 50 different octopus dishes since we opened Tipo. At the restaurant I like to use the really large octopus from Western Australia and sous vide the tentacles prior to chucking them on the grill. If I'm doing octopus at home, I cook it slowly in the oven with olive oil and herbs, let it rest for a while and then char it on the barbecue. The cooked octopus will keep well in the fridge for a few days, so you can make it ahead of time – just baste it with a little olive oil before refrigerating so it doesn't dry out. As salsa verde is such a versatile and delicious sauce to have on hand, I often make a bigger batch. It will last in the fridge for at least a week, ready to go with grilled meats or fish.

SERVES 4

400–500 g (14 oz–1 lb 2 oz)
    large octopus tentacles
2 tablespoons olive oil, plus
    extra for drizzling
1 small bay leaf
2 sprigs of thyme
2 black peppercorns
1 large leek, white part only
50 g (1¾ oz) unsalted butter
8 green olives, cheeks sliced
    from pits
sea salt

FOR THE SALSA VERDE
40 g (1½ oz) flat-leaf
    parsley leaves
125 ml (½ cup) olive oil
2½ tablespoons vegetable oil –
    or use basil oil or any other
    herb oil (see page 206)
4 anchovy fillets
3 teaspoons sherry vinegar
50 g (1¾ oz) capers
1 small clove of garlic,
    finely grated

For the salsa verde, put all the ingredients into a food processor and pulse to a rough, oily puree. Keep in the fridge until needed.

Preheat the oven to 120°C (235°F) fan-forced.

To prepare and cook the octopus, wash the tentacles with warm water to remove any excess slime and any grit that may be stuck in the suckers. Put the tentacles into an ovenproof dish with the olive oil, bay leaf, thyme and peppercorns and cover tightly with foil or a lid. Cook in the oven for 25 minutes.

Uncover the dish – the octopus will have released a lot of its juices; normally it loses over half its initial weight – and cut a small piece from the thicker part of the tentacle to try. If it's almost cooked to your liking, cover and leave to rest in its juices for another 10–15 minutes. The cooking time will depend on the size of the octopus and personal preference. I prefer chargrilled octopus to have a bit of bite, rather than a very soft, braised texture.

Remove the octopus from the dish, discarding the juices and spices, and set aside.

To prepare and cook the leek, cut the leek in half lengthwise, discarding the outer layer, then soak in cold water to remove any grit. It's best to leave the leek in the water for at least 10 minutes, then drain and pat dry with a clean tea towel. Place a frying pan over medium-low heat and melt the butter. When the butter is hot, lay in the leek, cut side down – if the leek is too long to fit in the pan, just cut it in half. Season with salt and cover with a lid.

The leek will start cooking in its own juices and butter, and eventually will start caramelising. Depending on the size of the leek, this should take 8–12 minutes; around 8 minutes in, take the lid off and check with a small knife to see if it is almost there. If it is tender but not caramelised, take off the lid and increase the heat, or if it is colouring too fast, just lower the heat.

Once the leek is cooked, cut it into 5–6 cm (2–2½ inch) lengths and set aside.

To chargrill the octopus, heat a barbecue or griddle pan to high and char the octopus for 1–2 minutes on each side. Cut each tentacle into 3–4 pieces, drizzle with olive oil and lightly season with salt.

To serve, spread the salsa verde over the plates, arrange the leek and octopus over the top and garnish with the green olives.

Calf's liver with balsamic onions

This is a very traditional Italian dish and was one of our menu mainstays at Tipo for many years. We don't have it on the menu now, but we still get regulars calling us and saying, 'We have a booking next Friday, can you please put the liver on?' And so we order a kilo or so in for them and serve it as a special that day. People who love liver really love this liver – the sweet and sour onions made with balsamic vinegar are a perfect match for the liver's earthiness. Make sure you cut the liver into thick slices, because the key with any liver is not to overcook it: keep it medium-rare, medium at most. This dish is great served with soft polenta.

SERVES 4

300 g (10½ oz) calf's liver
2–3 tablespoons vegetable oil
50 g (1¾ oz) unsalted butter
1 tablespoon finely chopped
    flat-leaf parsley leaves
plain (all-purpose) flour,
    for dusting
sea salt and freshly
    ground pepper

FOR THE BALSAMIC ONIONS
1 large brown onion, thinly sliced
3 tablespoons olive oil
200 ml (7 fl oz) balsamic vinegar
100 ml (3½ fl oz) chicken stock
1 teaspoon sugar, if needed

For the balsamic onions, slowly cook the onion in the olive oil over medium-low heat until soft and translucent, about 15 minutes. Season with salt, add the balsamic and cook for 15–20 minutes until the balsamic is reduced and starts caramelising. Add the stock, bring back to a simmer and cook for 10 minutes. Give it a taste – depending on the acidity of the vinegar, you may need to add a teaspoon of sugar. Set aside until needed. It will last in the fridge for at least 1 week.

To prepare the liver, use a small knife to peel off the thin membrane that coats the outer part of the liver as best you can, then cut the liver into large pieces about 1.5–2 cm ($^5/_8$–$^3/_4$ inches) thick, removing any sinew you may find. Season with salt and pepper and dust with a little flour.

Place a large non-stick frying pan over high heat, add the vegetable oil and cook the liver for 1 minute on one side, then turn and cook on the other side for 30 seconds. Remove the liver from the pan and reduce the heat to medium, then add the onions and butter and bring to a simmer. When the butter has emulsified, toss through the liver and parsley for 30 seconds, so the liver is well coated, then serve immediately.

Buffalo mozzarella with pistachio pesto & gnocco fritto

If you can find Italian buffalo mozzarella from Campania, you won't regret splashing out – it is very different from mozzarella from any other place in the world. When using pistachios (or any other nuts) in your cooking, go for the best you can afford: Iranian and Sicilian pistachios are always high quality. If you have any of the pistachio pesto left over, or you're making it in advance, store it in an airtight container in the fridge, with some plastic film pressed directly onto its surface so it doesn't oxidise and discolour – it will keep for up to 4 days. Gnocco fritto is traditionally served with salumi, but here the crispness of the fried dough squares makes a welcome contrast to the milky softness of the mozzarella.

SERVES 4

1 x 125 g (4½ oz) ball
    of buffalo mozzarella,
    torn into 2 or 3 pieces
olive oil and freshly ground
    pepper, to finish

FOR THE GNOCCO FRITTO
6 g (⅛ oz) fresh yeast or
    2.5 g (1/16 oz) active dried yeast
45 ml (1½ fl oz) lukewarm water
125 g (4½ oz) '00' flour
1 teaspoon sea salt
pinch of sugar
25 ml (¾ fl oz) olive oil
vegetable oil, for deep-frying

FOR THE PESTO
25 g (1 oz) basil leaves
75 ml (2½ fl oz) vegetable oil
25 ml (¾ fl oz) olive oil
75 g (2½ oz) coarsely ground
    pistachios
25 g (¼ cup) finely
    grated parmesan
sea salt

First make the dough for the gnocco fritto. In a small bowl or jug, mix the yeast with the lukewarm water until dissolved. In a stand mixer fitted with the hook attachment, mix the flour, salt and sugar with the yeast mixture on medium speed for 3 minutes. Add the olive oil and mix for 2 more minutes until the dough is smooth and elastic. Put into a clean bowl, cover with plastic film or reusable food wrap and leave to prove for 1–2 hours, or until the dough doubles in size.

In the meantime, for the pesto, put the basil and both oils into a food processor and blend until smooth, then add the pistachios and parmesan and pulse to a rough texture. Season with salt.

On a flour-dusted bench, or with a pasta machine, roll out the dough to 2–3 mm (⅛ inch) thick. (The dough is quite soft and can easily be rolled with a rolling pin, but I prefer to use the pasta machine to get a more even thickness.) Cut the rolled-out dough into 6–8 cm (2½–3¼ inch) squares.

To fry the gnocco fritto, pour about 5 cm (2 in) of vegetable oil into a deep saucepan and heat to 180°C (350°F). (To check the temperature without a thermometer, drop a small piece of dough into the oil – it should bubble up to the surface and start frying immediately.) Drop in as many pieces of dough as your pan can comfortably hold and fry until golden brown, about 1 minute on each side. Remove with a slotted spoon and drain on paper towel. Repeat until all the dough is used.

To serve, spoon the pesto onto a plate, top with the mozzarella and finish with a drizzle of olive oil and some pepper. Offer the gnocco fritto alongside.

Porchetta with pickled celeriac & sorrel

Not only is this a great Sunday roast, made more interesting by the pickled celeriac and the sauce, but any leftovers make the best sandwiches the next day. While the overnight marinade here is really spot on, if you're short of time you can buy porchetta already marinated and rolled from some butchers.

SERVES 4-6

1 x 800 g–1 kg (1 lb 12 oz–2 lb 4 oz) free-range pork belly, boneless
1 x 150 g (5½ oz) piece of pork loin
about 10 sorrel leaves
olive oil
sea salt

FOR THE MARINADE
12 g (1½ teaspoons) fine salt
1 teaspoon chilli flakes
1 tablespoon fennel seeds
4 cloves of garlic, coarsely chopped
1 tablespoon finely chopped sage leaves
1 tablespoon finely chopped rosemary leaves
50 ml (1½ fl oz) dry white wine

FOR THE PICKLED CELERIAC
1 small celeriac
150 ml (5 fl oz) dry white wine
150 ml (5 fl oz) white wine vinegar
100 g (3½ oz) caster (superfine) sugar
1 teaspoon fennel seeds
3–4 black peppercorns
2 sprigs of thyme

FOR THE SAUCE
1 small brown onion, thinly sliced
1 tablespoon vegetable oil
1 litre (4 cups) chicken stock or water
1 clove of garlic, crushed
2 sprigs of thyme
1 bay leaf
50 g (1¾ oz) unsalted butter

For the marinade, mix all the ingredients together to make a wet rub. Spread it evenly on the flesh side of the pork belly, trying to keep the skin dry. Leave to marinate in the fridge, uncovered and skin side up, overnight.

To make the pickled celeriac, peel the celeriac, keeping the skin for the sauce. Cut the celeriac in half and cut it into slices 1–2 mm (¹/₁₆ inch) thick – use a mandoline, if you have one. Put the wine, vinegar, sugar, spices and thyme into a small, non-aluminum pan with 150 ml (5 fl oz) of water and simmer for 5 minutes, then pour it over the sliced celeriac and cover. Let it pickle in the liquid until completely cold, then refrigerate until needed – it will keep well for a few days.

When you're ready to cook the porchetta, preheat the oven to 100°C (200°F) fan-forced.

Trim the pork loin so it will fit lengthwise inside the belly. Arrange over the flesh side of the pork belly and roll up as tightly as possible, using string to tie it securely every 1.5–2 cm (¾ inch) along its length. Put the porchetta on a wire rack in a roasting tin and pour a 1 cm (½ inch) depth of water into the tin. Cook in the oven for 2½–3½ hours, or until the meat's core temperature is 64°C (147°F); start checking with a probe thermometer after 2 hours.

While the porchetta is roasting, make the sauce. In a large frying pan over medium-high heat, saute the onion and the reserved celeriac skin in the vegetable oil until they're well browned, almost burnt. Transfer to a saucepan and cover with the chicken stock or water, garlic, thyme and bay leaf. Bring to the boil, then simmer for 1–2 hours until the liquid has reduced to 200–300 ml (7–10½ fl oz). Strain the reduction through a fine sieve into a clean pan and bring back to a simmer. Stir in the butter and 2–3 tablespoons of the liquid from the pickled celeriac, season with salt and simmer for 1–2 minutes until emulsified.

Once the thermometer registers the right core temperature, remove the porchetta and turn the oven up to 250°C (480°F). When the oven has reached temperature, return the meat and cook for 10 minutes, then rotate the tin and cook for another 10 minutes or until the skin is puffed up and really crispy. Let the porchetta rest for about 10–15 minutes before removing the twine.

To serve, cut the porchetta into slices about 2–3 cm (1 inch) thick and place a slice on each plate. Spoon some sauce around it, then top with 5–6 slices of the pickled celeriac, a few sorrel leaves and a generous drizzle of olive oil.

Pictured overleaf

LUKE'S WINE MATCHES

To balance the super-rich porchetta, I'm looking for a wine with high acidity – one that will play a similar role to the pickled celeriac in the dish. Wines from one of my favourite regions of Italy for nebbiolo, Valtellina, fit the bill. Filled with vibrant red fruit and lively acidity, these wines live for a long time, so don't be scared to choose a bottle with some age behind it!

Porchetta with pickled celeriac & sorrel (see previous page)

Tipomisu *and* Other Desserts

Tipomisu

Our signature dessert is a collaboration with my friend Anthony Hart, who's a pastry chef and photographer. In fact, he first came up with the idea of calling it Tipomisu, which initially seemed a bit corny, but I soon realised it was genius. I was talking to him about how I wanted to do a version of tiramisu that included a chocolate brownie and a mascarpone cream I was working on. Anthony has amazing skills with chocolate and suggested using a disc of tempered chocolate as one of the layers. He even made the chocolate discs for us in the early days. If you're less comfortable with tempering chocolate, you can just use melted chocolate for the discs. There's also an espresso and chocolate salted caramel, making this a very rich, very chocolatey dessert – and a long recipe, but you can get a head start by making the brownie and the chocolate discs the day before. Save any offcuts of brownie or chocolate from the discs to mix with some ice-cream.

SERVES 8

FOR THE CHOCOLATE BROWNIE
250 g (9 oz) dark chocolate (70% cocoa)
115 g (4 oz) unsalted butter
3 large whole eggs
225 g (8 oz) brown sugar
1 vanilla bean, split and seeds scraped
50 g (1¾ oz) '00' or plain (all-purpose) flour
25 g (1 oz) rye flour
1 tablespoon cocoa powder

FOR THE CHOCOLATE DISCS
250 g (9 oz) dark chocolate (70% cocoa)

For the chocolate brownie, preheat the oven to 170°C (325°F) and line a 25 cm (10 inch) square baking tin with baking paper.

In a heatproof bowl, melt the chocolate and butter set over a saucepan of simmering water (make sure the base of the bowl doesn't touch the water) until completely melted and emulsified.

In the meantime, place the eggs, brown sugar and vanilla seeds in the bowl of a mixer fitted with the whisk attachment and whisk on medium-high speed until pale, then reduce the speed and slowly add the warm chocolate and butter mixture. Once fully incorporated, remove the bowl from the mixer and fold in the flours and cocoa with a rubber spatula until just combined, being careful not to overmix.

Pour the brownie batter into the tin and bake for 20–25 minutes, or until a knife inserted into the centre of the brownie comes out clean. Leave to cool to room temperature, then chill in the fridge for several hours or overnight.

For the discs, temper the chocolate by melting three-quarters of it in a heatproof bowl set over a saucepan of simmering water (make sure the base of the bowl doesn't touch the water).

In the meantime, for the brownie, finely chop the remaining chocolate. When the melting chocolate has reached 35°C (95°F), remove the bowl from the pan and add the chopped chocolate, stirring until the temperature cools to 27°C (80°F), then gently reheat over the simmering water until the temperature reaches 31–32°C (88–90°F). Otherwise, you can just melt the chocolate.

FOR THE MASCARPONE CREAM
4 egg yolks
65 g (2¼ oz) icing
    (confectioners') sugar
400 g (14 oz) mascarpone cheese
140 ml (4½ fl oz) cream (35% fat)
1 tablespoon dark rum

FOR THE CARAMEL
125 ml (½ cup) cream (35% fat)
125 g (4½ oz) caster
    (superfine) sugar
2 shots of strong espresso
1 teaspoon sea salt
50 g (1¾ oz) dark chocolate
    (70% cocoa)

Spread the chocolate onto acetate or baking paper to make a sheet approximately 1 mm (¹⁄₁₆ inch) thick. Once it's partially set, use an 8 cm (3¼ inch) ring cutter to cut out 8 discs, then allow the chocolate to fully set for 3–4 hours, or preferably overnight.

Carefully remove the discs from the acetate or baking paper and place in an airtight container with baking paper between each one and store in a cool place – but not the fridge – until needed. (However, if you melted the chocolate rather than tempering it, you could refrigerate the discs to try to imitate the 'snap' of tempered chocolate.)

For the mascarpone cream, place all the ingredients except the dark rum into the bowl of a stand mixer fitted with the whisk attachment. Whisk until smooth and thick – you're after medium peaks that will hold their shape fairly well – then add the rum and whisk lightly, just to mix through the rum. Place the mascarpone cream into a piping bag fitted with a 5 mm (¼ inch) nozzle and keep in the fridge until needed.

To make the caramel, heat the cream in a small saucepan to just below simmering point. In a heavy-based saucepan, melt the sugar over medium heat, without stirring, until you have a golden-brown caramel, then slowly add the cream – be careful, as it could splatter and overflow if you pour in too much cream at once. Once the cream is fully incorporated, let it boil for 1 minute, then add the espresso and salt and bring back to the boil. Take off the heat and whisk in the chocolate until smooth. Pass the caramel through a fine sieve into a jug and keep warm.

When ready to assemble, turn out the brownie onto a chopping board. With an 8 cm (3¼ inch) ring cutter, cut out 8 discs, then use a 6 cm (2½ inch) ring cutter to remove the centre of each brownie disc to form a ring.

Place a brownie ring in the centre of a plate and fill the centre with mascarpone cream. Put a chocolate disc on top, then dust generously with cocoa powder. Pipe three dollops of the mascarpone cream on top of the chocolate disc and two larger ones on either side. Spoon about 2 tablespoons of the warm caramel in the centre of the disc and serve immediately.

Pictured overleaf

Tipomisu (see previous page)

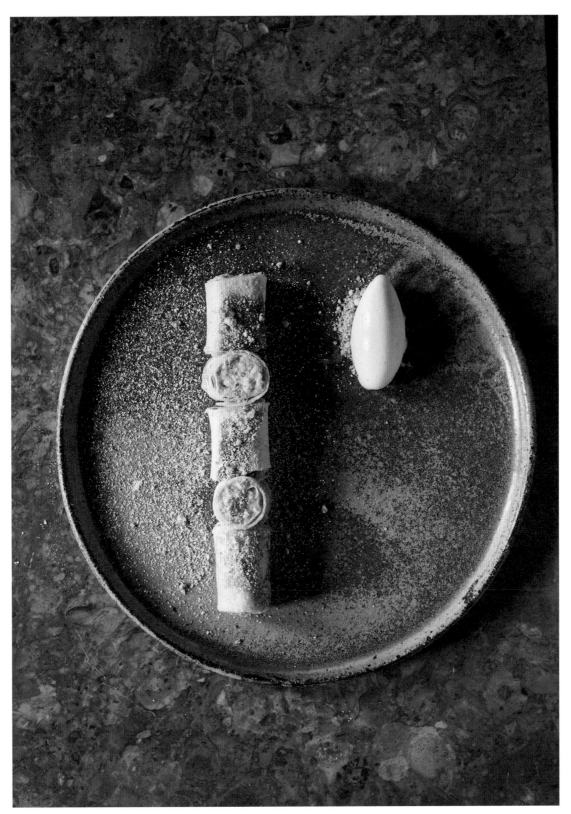

Crespella with ricotta & pistachio (see overleaf)

Crespella with ricotta & pistachio

A crespella is essentially an Italian crepe. You make the crepes, fill them with a frangipane and ricotta mixture, then roll up into cigars and bake in the oven. This has great texture and flavour, but it's not too sweet – a very Tipo kind of dessert.

SERVES 8

FOR THE FRANGIPANE
100 g (3½ oz) unsalted butter, softened
100 g (3½ oz) caster (superfine) sugar
2 small eggs
100 g (3½ oz) almond meal
25 g (1 oz) plain (all-purpose) flour

FOR THE PASTRY CREAM
200 ml (7 fl oz) whole milk
50 g (1¾ oz) egg yolk (from about 3 eggs)
40 g (1½ oz) caster (superfine) sugar
15 g (½ oz) plain (all-purpose) flour
15 g (½ oz) cornflour (cornstarch)

FOR THE CREPES
100 g (3½ oz) plain (all-purpose) flour
25 g (1 oz) caster (superfine) sugar
2 medium eggs
225 ml (7¾ fl oz) whole milk
vegetable oil spray, for frying

TO FINISH
125 g (4½ oz) pistachios
500 g (1 lb 2 oz) ricotta
icing (confectioners') sugar, for dusting
fior di latte or pistachio gelato, to serve

For the frangipane, preheat the oven to 160°C (315°F) and line a baking tray with baking paper.

Place the softened butter and caster sugar in the bowl of a stand mixer fitted with the paddle attachment and beat on high speed until pale. Add the eggs one at a time, beating well between each addition, then add the almond meal and flour and mix until just incorporated. Spread the mixture onto the baking tray and bake for 15 minutes or until golden and cooked through. Allow to cool.

To make the pastry cream, place all the ingredients in a small saucepan and whisk well. Keep whisking over low heat to cook out the pastry cream until it begins to thicken, then remove from the heat and allow to cool.

To make the crepes, place all the ingredients except the vegetable oil in a bowl and use either a whisk or stick blender to mix to a smooth batter.

Place a non-stick frying pan over medium heat, lightly spray with vegetable oil and pour about 2 tablespoons of the batter into the middle of the pan. Quickly, with a twisting circular movement, tilt the pan to spread the batter evenly. Once the crepe is dry on the top, flip it over and cook the other side for about 30 seconds. Continue the same process with the rest of the batter – you should have about 8–10 crepes.

To finish, use a blender or pestle and mortar to finely grind the pistachios. Save some for the garnish and put the rest into a large bowl. Crumble in the cooled frangipane, then add the cooled pastry cream and the ricotta and mix well.

Preheat the oven to 180°C (350°F) and line a baking tray with baking paper.

Spoon or pipe a strip of filling along the top third of each crepe, then roll into a log. Place the filled crespelle on the baking tray and bake for 10 minutes, just to heat through.

Cut each crespella into 4–5 pieces, dust with icing sugar and sprinkle with the reserved ground pistachios. Serve with fior di latte or pistachio gelato.

Pictured on previous page

Mandarin panna cotta with oat crumble

I love this because it's not your traditional panna cotta recipe that's all about the cream. I mix in some mandarin puree to make it lighter and fresher. Virtually any kind of fruit or vegetable puree would also work – orange, carrot, berries, passionfruit, rhubarb, whatever. This panna cotta is quick to make and always sets perfectly overnight.

SERVES 8

250 ml (1 cup) whole milk
100 g (3½ oz) caster (superfine) sugar
25 g (1 oz) honey
3 sprigs of mountain marigold, lemon verbena, lemon thyme or lemon myrtle, plus extra leaves to garnish
5 gold-strength gelatine leaves
250 ml (1 cup) cream (35% fat), chilled
mandarin segments, to serve

FOR THE MANDARIN PUREE
4–6 mandarins, peeled

FOR THE CRUMBLE
125 g (4½ oz) rye flour
40 g (1½ oz) rolled oats
75 g (2½ oz) unsalted butter, diced
50 g (1¾ oz) white chocolate
50 g (1¾ oz) brown sugar

For the mandarin puree, blend the mandarins until smooth, then pass through a sieve – you need to end up with 250 ml (1 cup) puree for the panna cotta, plus enough extra for the garnish.

To make the panna cotta, bring the milk, caster sugar, honey and herb sprigs to the boil. Remove from the heat, cover and leave to infuse for 15–20 minutes.

Meanwhile, soak the gelatine leaves in cold water for 15 minutes.

Discard the herb sprigs from the infused milk mixture and bring it back to the boil. Add the squeezed-out gelatine and stir to dissolve completely.

Save a little of the mandarin puree to garnish, then mix the rest into the infused milk, along with the cream, emulsifying with a stick blender until smooth. Divide the panna cotta mixture evenly between 8 dariole moulds and allow to set overnight in the fridge.

For the crumble, preheat the oven to 170°C (325°F) and line a baking tray with baking paper.

Place the flour and oats in a bowl. Melt the butter in a frying pan over medium heat and cook until the milk solids start turning brown and have a nutty aroma. Take off the heat and allow to cool.

Put the white chocolate and brown sugar into a heatproof bowl and set over a saucepan of simmering water (make sure the base of the bowl doesn't touch the water), then stir until melted and combined. Add the cooled brown butter and mix to combine.

Now add the chocolate mixture to the flour and oats and mix well with a spatula. Spread the crumble evenly over the baking tray and bake for 15 minutes – if the sides start to caramelise first, give the crumble a stir to avoid burning.

To serve, briefly submerge the base of each mould in a bowl of hot water to loosen the panna cotta, then carefully turn out onto a plate. Garnish with the crumble, reserved mandarin puree, a few mandarin segments and some extra herb leaves.

White chocolate & fig leaf mousse with berries

This dessert is all about the fig-leaf-infused cream. Fig leaves impart a herbaceous flavour to sweet dishes unlike anything else. Make sure you wash the fig leaves thoroughly before you use them and strip out any woody stems; you'll also need a high-speed blender to reduce the leaves to a puree. At the restaurant, we finish this dessert with a fig leaf oil. If you want to try that, just substitute fig leaves for the herbs in the herb oil recipe on page 206, or you could use basil oil instead if you have some to hand.

SERVES 8

725 ml (25 fl oz) cream (35% fat)
50 g (1¾ oz) fig leaves, stems removed, well washed, then chopped
1½ gold-strength gelatine leaves
40 g (1½ oz) liquid glucose
125 g (4½ oz) white chocolate
mixed berries, to serve
fig leaf or basil oil, to serve – optional (see recipe introduction)

To infuse the cream, bring 400 ml (14 fl oz) of the cream and the fig leaves to the boil in a small saucepan, then take off the heat, cover and leave to infuse for 30 minutes.

Soak the gelatine leaves in cold water for 15 minutes.

Meanwhile, transfer the infused cream to a high-speed blender and blend for 2 minutes to break down all the fibres, then strain into a clean pan and discard the fig leaves.

Add the glucose to the infused cream and bring to the boil. Squeeze out excess water from the gelatine, then stir into the cream mixture to dissolve completely. Add the white chocolate and emulsify with a stick blender or hand whisk until smooth. Finally, add the remaining 325 ml (11 fl oz) cream and blend again, just to combine. Strain into a clean container and leave to set in the fridge overnight.

Before serving, whisk the mousse to a whipped cream consistency, then spoon into bowls and serve with the berries and some fig leaf or basil oil, if you like.

Ricotta bombolone with fennel cream

This is not a classic bombolone recipe – that is made with a more brioche-style dough. Ours is more like a zeppoli dough, which includes heaps of ricotta, resulting in a crunchy shell and a soft centre. These are really good for making at home: very simple, very quick and very impressive.

SERVES 8

250 g (9 oz) ricotta
70 g (2½ oz) caster (superfine) sugar, plus extra for dusting
4 whole eggs
250 g (9 oz) plain (all-purpose) flour
10 g (¼ oz) baking powder
finely grated zest of 1 orange
vegetable oil, for deep-frying

FOR THE FENNEL CREAM
250 g (9 oz) cream (35% fat)
1 tablespoon fennel seeds
25 g (1 oz) icing (confectioner's) sugar

For the fennel cream, bring the cream and fennel seeds to the boil in a small saucepan, then remove from the heat, cover and allow to infuse for 30 minutes. Strain the infused cream through a sieve and discard the fennel seeds. Chill in the fridge until completely cold.

To make the bombolone dough, put the ricotta and caster sugar into the bowl of a stand mixer fitted with the paddle attachment and beat on medium-high speed until smooth, approximately 5 minutes. Add the eggs one at a time, beating well between each addition. Lastly add the flour, baking powder and orange zest and mix for a minute, just until smooth. Transfer the dough to a piping bag.

Prepare the extra caster sugar, ready to roll your cooked bombolone in.

To fry the bombolone, pour about 5 cm (2 in) of oil into a deep saucepan and heat to 180°C (350°F). (To check the temperature without a thermometer, drop a small piece of dough into the oil – it should bubble up to the surface and start frying immediately.) Cut a 2 cm (¾ inch) hole at the pointed end of the piping bag. Holding the piping bag only a few centimetres (about an inch) above the oil, carefully pipe 2–3 cm (¾–1¼ inch) long pieces of dough. Use kitchen scissors to cut off each length of dough from the piping bag and fry until golden, 4–5 minutes. Repeat until all the dough is used – but try not to overcrowd the pan, so the temperature of the oil doesn't drop too much. Using a slotted spoon, remove the cooked bombolone and immediately roll in the extra sugar.

While the bombolone are frying, take the fennel cream from the fridge, add the icing sugar and whisk to soft peaks. Serve with the hot bombolone.

Whipped sorrel cheesecake with rhubarb

This starts like a traditional baked cheesecake that you bake almost to the point of being overcooked. You then let it cool and set. Once it has done so, you blitz it in a food processor with heaps of sorrel, so it turns a beautiful green colour and is smooth, like a mousse. Amazing, especially when you team it with rhubarb. An aged balsamic or balsamic glaze compliments the dish really well too.

SERVES 8

225 g (8 oz) full-fat
   cream cheese
190 g (6¾ oz) caster
   (superfine) sugar
880 g (1 lb 15 oz) ricotta
3 whole eggs
1 tbsp cornflour (cornstarch)
1 vanilla bean, split and
   seeds scraped
finely grated zest of 1 orange
1 capful of amaretto, or a few
   drops of almond extract
120 g (4¼ oz) French sorrel,
   stems removed, leaves
   well washed and dried

FOR THE RHUBARB
50 g (1¾ oz) caster
   (superfine) sugar
1 teaspoon sea salt
250 g (9 oz) rhubarb,
   well washed, then
   trimmed and cut into
   2 cm (¾ inch) lengths

Preheat the oven to 170°C (325°F) and line a baking tray with baking paper.

To make the cheesecake, place the cream cheese and sugar in the bowl of a stand mixer fitted with the paddle attachment and beat on medium-high speed to remove any lumps, then add the ricotta and keep beating until smooth. Add the eggs one at a time, beating well between each addition. Lastly add the cornflour, vanilla seeds, orange zest and amaretto or almond extract and mix on low speed, just to combine.

Pour the cheesecake mixture into the baking tray and bake for 40–50 minutes, or until firm and golden brown on top, then allow to cool completely.

Place your cooled cheesecake into a blender with the sorrel and blend until smooth. Be careful not to overdo it, as the sorrel will turn brown if the mixture gets too warm during the blending.

For the rhubarb, place the sugar and salt into a non-aluminium pan with 50 ml (1½ fl oz) of water and simmer to make a syrup. Add the rhubarb and cook over low heat until tender and reduced, about 6–8 minutes, then allow to cool.

Serve a large spoonful of the cheesecake mousse alongside some rhubarb.

Rice pudding with figs & vincotto

This simple rice pudding is very comforting. It's also a perfect fuss-free dessert for making ahead of time when you're having friends around for lunch or dinner. I love the combination of figs and vincotto to go with it, but some fresh raspberries work well too.

SERVES 4

500 ml (2 cups) whole milk
50 g (1¾ oz) risotto rice,
    preferably Carnaroli
50 g (1¾ oz) caster
    (superfine) sugar
1 sprig of rosemary
1 small cinnamon stick
pinch of sea salt
25 g (1 oz) white chocolate
100 ml (3½ fl oz) cream (35% fat)
2 tablespoons vincotto
4 fresh figs, sliced

To make the rice pudding, in a heavy-based saucepan, bring the milk to a simmer, then stir in the rice, sugar, rosemary, cinnamon and salt. Cook over the lowest possible heat for about 45 minutes, stirring frequently, until the texture is thick and creamy like a risotto, and the rice is well cooked. Remove the rosemary and cinnamon, then add the white chocolate and stir until it has melted. Transfer the rice pudding to a clean container and chill in the fridge until completely cold.

Whip the cream to soft peaks, then gently fold into the cold rice pudding in two or three stages. (If you're making this in advance, it can now be kept in the fridge for 3–4 days.)

When you're ready to serve, spoon the rice pudding onto plates, drizzle with the vincotto and arrange some sliced figs on top.

Basics *and* Other Essentials

Herb oil

At Tipo we use infused oils to achieve super-intense flavours in our dishes. This one is deeply herbaceous, making it great for finishing antipasti or adding to white pasta sauces, such as the one in the spaghetti with marron & finger lime on page 60. I have given specific amounts for the perfect ratio here, but you don't have to be so pedantic, and if you have too much of something in your herb garden, you could happily substitute with other herbs.

MAKES ABOUT 200 ML (7 FL OZ)

40 g (1½ oz) flat-leaf
    parsley leaves
20 g (¾ oz) basil leaves
10 g (¼ oz) tarragon leaves
10 g (¼ oz) mint leaves
250 ml (1 cup) vegetable oil

Blanch all the herb leaves in boiling water for 10 seconds, then refresh in iced water (this helps to retain their bright green colour). Drain the leaves, transfer to a clean tea towel and squeeze out as much water as possible.

In a small saucepan, warm the oil to 60–65°C (140–150°F).

Blend the herb leaves and warm oil in a high-speed blender for 4–5 minutes until the oil is very green and smooth. Strain through a conical sieve lined with a paper coffee filter, then pour into a clean jar and chill before using; the herb oil will keep in the fridge for up to 2 weeks.

Basil oil

We use this oil to drizzle on our focaccia (see page 212), but its clean, fresh flavour makes it versatile enough to finish many dishes.

MAKES ABOUT 200 ML (7 FL OZ)

40 g (1½ oz) basil leaves
200 ml (7 fl oz) vegetable oil

Blanch the basil leaves in boiling water for 10 seconds, then refresh in iced water (this helps to retain their bright green colour). Drain the leaves, transfer to a clean tea towel and squeeze out as much water as possible.

Blend the basil with the oil in a high-speed blender, or with a stick blender, for 2–3 minutes. Strain through a conical sieve lined with a paper coffee filter, then pour into a clean jar and chill before using; the basil oil will keep in the fridge for up to 2 weeks.

Nettle oil

Intense on its own, this unique oil is best used in white-wine-based ragus, such as the rabbit ones on pages 54 and 84, to give them an extra dimension.

MAKES ABOUT 200 ML (7 FL OZ)

75 g (2½ oz) nettle leaves (wear gloves when picking)
small handful of baby spinach leaves – optional
250 ml (1 cup) vegetable oil

Nettles and spinach can be really gritty, so make sure you soak them in plenty of cold water to flush out any grit or soil, then rinse in several changes of water. Spin the leaves in a salad spinner or pat dry with a tea towel.

In a small saucepan, warm the oil to 60–65°C (140–150°F).

Blend the nettles, spinach and warm oil in a high-speed blender for 4–5 minutes until the oil is very green and smooth. Strain through a conical sieve lined with a paper coffee filter, then pour into a clean jar and chill before using; the nettle oil will keep in the fridge for up to 2 weeks.

Bitter leaves & balsamic

I love the intense flavour of bitter greens almost as much as I love Campari. Just buy whatever bitter leaves you can get from your local market, balancing their bitterness with the sweetness of baby cos lettuce.

SERVES 4

1 small head of radicchio
1 witlof (chicory)
1 bunch of curly endive (frisee)
1 head of baby cos
sea salt

FOR THE DRESSING
25 ml (¾ fl oz) balsamic vinegar
1 small clove of garlic, bruised
125 ml (½ cup) olive oil

For the dressing, put the balsamic and the garlic into a bowl, then slowly whisk in the olive oil until combined. Let the garlic clove infuse the dressing for 30 minutes, then discard it – this adds an element of complexity to the dressing without the garlic flavour becoming overpowering.

Tear or cut all the large leaves into chunks, then wash thoroughly in cold water. Dry well, then transfer to a bowl, season with a little salt and dress generously with the dressing.

If you have any leftover dressing, keep it in a screw-top jar in the fridge, where it will last for at least 2 weeks.

House dressing

This 'agrodolce', or sweet and sour, dressing goes well with pretty much any salad leaves or steamed vegetables. The mustard and honey also act as emulsifiers to give you a thick and luscious dressing, and the vinegar adds sharpness.

SERVES 4

25 ml (¾ fl oz) sherry vinegar
30 g (1 oz) Dijon mustard
30 g (1 oz) honey
pinch of sea salt, or
    more to taste
125 ml (½ cup) vegetable oil
100 ml (3½ fl oz) olive oil

Put the vinegar, mustard, honey and salt into a bowl and whisk to dissolve the salt, then slowly whisk in the oils until the dressing is thick and emulsified.

If you have any leftover dressing, keep it in a screw-top jar in the fridge, where it will last for at least 2 weeks.

Mayonnaise

This is my straightforward, easy-to-make mayonnaise.
I make it with a whole egg so there's no waste and the
resulting mayonnaise is very stable – I use a stick blender
for this, which takes minutes, and it never splits.

**MAKES ABOUT 250 G
(9 OZ)**

1 whole egg
1 teaspoon Dijon mustard
2 tablespoons lemon juice
150 ml (5 fl oz) vegetable oil
50 ml (1½ fl oz) olive oil
sea salt

Put all the ingredients into a jug or bowl wide enough to fit
the stick blender and blend on high speed until emulsified
into a mayonnaise.

Keep in the fridge and use within 48 hours.

Pangrattato

This is the pangrattato we sprinkle over our orecchiette with cime di rapa (see page 146) at Tipo, but it's excellent with many other pastas, including the simple aglio, olio e peperoncino on page 155. Don't be tempted to skip the big, absorbent panko breadcrumbs – they make all the difference – and if your pasta sauce contains anchovy, you could also substitute some of the olive oil with oil from the tin or jar of anchovies. As pangrattato can be sprinkled on top of pretty much any pasta, and it keeps well, I tend to make a big batch and keep it in a jar to use throughout the week.

MAKES ABOUT 100 G (3½ OZ)

50 g (1¾ oz) panko breadcrumbs
40–50 ml (1¼–1½ fl oz) olive oil
2 tablespoons finely grated parmesan
finely grated zest of 1 lemon
sea salt

Preheat a non-stick frying pan over medium-low heat and slowly toast the breadcrumbs until they start to turn golden brown.

Add the oil progressively, in two or three batches, and keep tossing the breadcrumbs until they start frying, about 2 minutes. Take off the heat, add the parmesan and lemon zest and season with salt.

Leave the pangrattato to cool before storing in an airtight container for up to a week.

Focaccia

When I was planning the menu at Tipo, I did a lot of playing around with the focaccia recipe. I wanted a sourdough, crunchy style of focaccia, rather than a fluffy, white-bread style. At the restaurant we use a sourdough 'mother' that's ten years old, but I've adapted this version to be quicker and easier to make at home. You'll need to make the pre-ferment the day before, but you can then mix the dough the morning of the next day, and it will be ready to bake in the afternoon. We serve our focaccia with basil oil (see page 206) and fresh ricotta.

SERVES 6

7 g (¼ oz) fresh yeast – or
   3 g (¹⁄₁₆ oz) active dried yeast
400 ml (14 fl oz) lukewarm water
615 g (1 lb 5½ oz) '00' flour
18 g (¾ oz) fine salt
olive oil
2 handfuls of coarsely
   chopped mixed herbs
sea salt

FOR THE PRE-FERMENT
1 g (0.03 oz) fresh yeast – or
   ½ teaspoon active dried yeast
350 ml (12 fl oz) lukewarm water
350 g (12 oz) '00' flour

For the pre-ferment, mix the yeast and water in a bowl until the yeast has dissolved; if using dried yeast, activate it in some of the lukewarm water beforehand, following the instructions on the package. Add the flour and mix with a spatula for 2 minutes to incorporate thoroughly. Cover the bowl with plastic film or reusable food wrap, or transfer the pre-ferment to an airtight container, and leave at room temperature for 2–3 hours to activate. When it is bubbly and active, move it to the fridge and chill overnight.

The next day, mix the dough. Start by dissolving or activating the yeast in the same way as you did for the pre-ferment. Now put the pre-ferment into the bowl of a stand mixer fitted with the hook attachment, then add the flour and salt. Pour the yeast mixture over the top and mix on low speed for 1 minute. Increase the speed to medium and continue mixing for 4–5 minutes until you have a soft, loose dough.

Transfer the dough to a well-oiled bowl and lightly oil the top of the dough as well, then cover with plastic film, pressing it directly onto the dough, and leave at room temperature to proof for 30 minutes.

The dough will be very soft and sticky, so having an oiled surface and hands helps a great deal when working the dough. Lightly oil a clean benchtop and tip the dough out of the bowl onto the bench. With oiled hands, take one side of the dough, stretch it and fold it over itself. Do the same on the other side, then turn the dough 90 degrees and repeat the process with both sides again.

Return the dough to the bowl and let it proof for 30–45 minutes – during this time, it will increase in size by about half – then repeat the same stretching and folding process. The second time the dough should have a lot more strength and elasticity, making it easier to work. Return the dough to the bowl and this time let it proof until doubled in size, about 45 minutes–1 hour, depending on the temperature; in winter, in a cold house, it could take as long as 2 hours.

Line a baking tray with baking paper, then generously drizzle with olive oil. Transfer the dough to the tray and let it relax for 15 minutes, then push the dough down with your fingers, stretching it to fill the tray. Drizzle some olive oil over the top and sprinkle with the herbs and some sea salt, then leave to proof for a final 15 minutes.

Meanwhile, preheat the oven to 220°C (425°F) fan-forced.

Bake the focaccia for about 25 minutes, or until it is cooked through and golden brown all over. Check on it 15–20 minutes in, and if the top is colouring too much, carefully flip it over in the tray.

Allow to cool on a wire rack before serving.

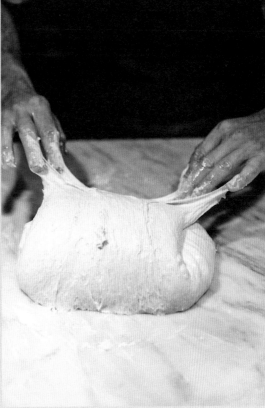

Focaccia (see previous page)

Chicken stock

I buy bags of chicken bones to make a big batch of stock, but I also use the carcasses from whole chickens I have roasted. You can even make a small amount of stock from the wings and any other scraps you've trimmed off before cooking chicken. All you need to do is simmer them in enough water to cover for about an hour or so – it doesn't take long and helps to ensure that you'll always have stock in the freezer.

MAKES ABOUT 2-3 LITRES (8-12 CUPS)

3 chicken carcasses
1 small brown onion, quartered
1 celery stalk, coarsely chopped
1 carrot, coarsely chopped
1 small bay leaf
2 sprigs of thyme
3–4 black peppercorns

Put the carcasses into a large saucepan that holds them comfortably and top up with cold water to cover, about 4 litres (16 cups). Bring to a slow simmer, using a slotted spoon to skim off any impurities that come to the top, then add the vegetables, herbs and peppercorns. Simmer over the lowest possible heat for 3 hours, skimming the fat from the top every half hour or so.

Strain the stock through a fine sieve, then either use right away or let it cool before storing in airtight containers in the fridge for up to 3 days or in the freezer for up to 3 months.

Fish stock

When I go to the markets for fish, rather than getting fillets, I buy the whole fish and ask the fishmonger to fillet it for me and then give me the bones and head to make stock. Fillets bought this way can work out cheaper, and are definitely fresher than fish that may have been filleted the day before. Most fishmongers also sell, or even give away, fish bones – those of any white fish are good for this stock.

MAKES ABOUT 2-3 LITRES (8-12 CUPS)

1–2 fish carcasses and heads
½ brown onion, thinly sliced
1 celery stalk, thinly sliced
½ fennel bulb, thinly sliced
1 small bay leaf
2 sprigs of thyme
½ lemon

To prepare the fish bones, use a pair of scissors to snip the gills from the heads, then remove any bloodline that's still attached to the spine. Wash the bones and heads really well with cold water, then put them into a pot that holds them comfortably. Top up with cold water, about 3–4 litres (12–16 cups), and bring to a slow simmer.

With a slotted spoon, skim off any impurities that come to the surface, then simmer for 30 minutes. Take off the heat and add the vegetables, herbs and lemon half, then cover with a lid and leave to infuse for 30 minutes.

Strain the stock through a fine sieve, then either use right away or let it cool before storing in airtight containers in the fridge for up to 3 days or in the freezer for up to 3 months.

BASICS AND OTHER ESSENTIALS

Vegetable stock

Stock is a great way to use any vegetables that are past their prime. The version here makes a really delicious broth that, with the addition of a little saffron, also becomes the perfect base for a risotto alla Milanese.

MAKES ABOUT 1.5 LITRES (6 CUPS)

1 large brown onion
1 carrot, peeled
1 celery stalk, around 100 g (3½ oz)
1 small leek, white part only
2 button mushrooms
½ small fennel bulb
3 tablespoons vegetable oil
1 tomato, seeds removed, coarsely chopped
a few flat-leaf parsley sprigs
3–4 black peppercorns
2 sprigs of thyme
1 small bay leaf

Slice all the vegetables (except the tomato) as thinly as possible – I like to use a mandoline for this.

Put the oil into a large saucepan over medium-low heat, add all the other ingredients and saute for about 20 minutes, trying not to let them get any colour. Top up with 2 litres (8 cups) of water, turn the heat down to low and simmer for 1 hour.

Strain the stock through a fine sieve, then either use right away or let it cool before storing in airtight containers in the fridge for up to 5 days, or in the freezer for up to 3 months.

Napoli tomato sauce

This is our basic Napoli sauce that we always have in the fridge at Tipo and use as the base for a lot of our sauces. At home, I make a big batch and freeze it in small containers.

MAKES ABOUT 2 LITRES (8 CUPS)

80 ml (⅓ cup) olive oil
1 brown onion, finely diced
2 cloves of garlic, crushed
3 x 400 g (14 oz) tins of
    peeled tomatoes, ideally
    San Marzano
basil leaves from 2–3 sprigs
sea salt

Heat the olive oil in a large saucepan over medium-low heat, then add the onion and garlic and cook until soft and translucent, around 6–8 minutes.

Add the tomatoes and stir well, then bring to a slow simmer. Turn the heat down to low and cook for 1 hour, stirring occasionally to make sure the sauce doesn't catch on the bottom.

Taste and season with salt, then take off the heat and let the sauce rest for 15 minutes before you add the basil.

We normally pass this sauce through a vegetable mill while it's still hot. If you don't have one, you can just use a whisk to crush the tomatoes – don't be tempted to blitz the sauce with a blender, or you'll lose its pleasingly rustic texture.

Pork & fennel sausage

You will, of course, need a mincer for this recipe (I use an inexpensive attachment for my stand mixer that is both mincer and filler), but it makes a relatively quick, basic sausage that can be ready to use in a sausage pasta or on a pizza the next day. I prefer to use pork neck meat, but shoulder works just as well, and the back fat retains good texture when it cooks, which makes for a better, juicier sausage. Obviously you can buy pretty good sausages, but it is hard to beat the satisfaction you will get when you hang your own homemade sausage in the fridge. Sausage-making is a great skill to have and, believe me, it sounds more challenging than it is.

MAKES 8 SAUSAGES

900 g (2 lb) pork neck
    or shoulder meat
300 g (10½ oz) pork back fat
20 g (¾ oz) fine salt
3 cloves of garlic,
    coarsely chopped
2 teaspoons fennel seeds
1 heaped teaspoon chilli flakes
2 tablespoons dried oregano
1 tablespoon freshly ground
    pepper
60 ml (¼ cup) dry vermouth
    or white wine
sausage casings – optional

Cut the pork meat and fat into chunks small enough to go through your mincer. Put the meat and fat into a bowl and mix with all the remaining ingredients except the casings, then cover and leave to marinate in the fridge overnight.

The next day, set up your mincer with the largest die it comes with, ideally 8–10 mm (³⁄₈–¹⁄₂ inch), and mince all the meat and fat into a bowl. Mix well with your hands for 1–2 minutes to combine thoroughly.

At this stage, you can use the mix as is for a sausage pasta or store it in batches, in airtight containers, in the fridge for 4–5 days, or in the freezer for up to 2 months.

Alternatively, if you have a sausage filler attachment for your mixer, you can use that to stuff the sausage meat into casings. Put the casings around the funnel at the front of the filler, start the machine and feed it with the sausage meat. Try to be constantly feeding the meat, so there won't be any air bubbles in the sausages. Push it all through as one long sausage and then twist into lengths every 10–12 cm (4–4½ inches). It is best to hang the finished sausages in the fridge to dry for 1–3 days before you cook them. This makes them less likely to burst, as well as giving them a fuller, more matured flavour.

These sausages will keep in the fridge for up to 5 days, or in the freezer for 2 months.

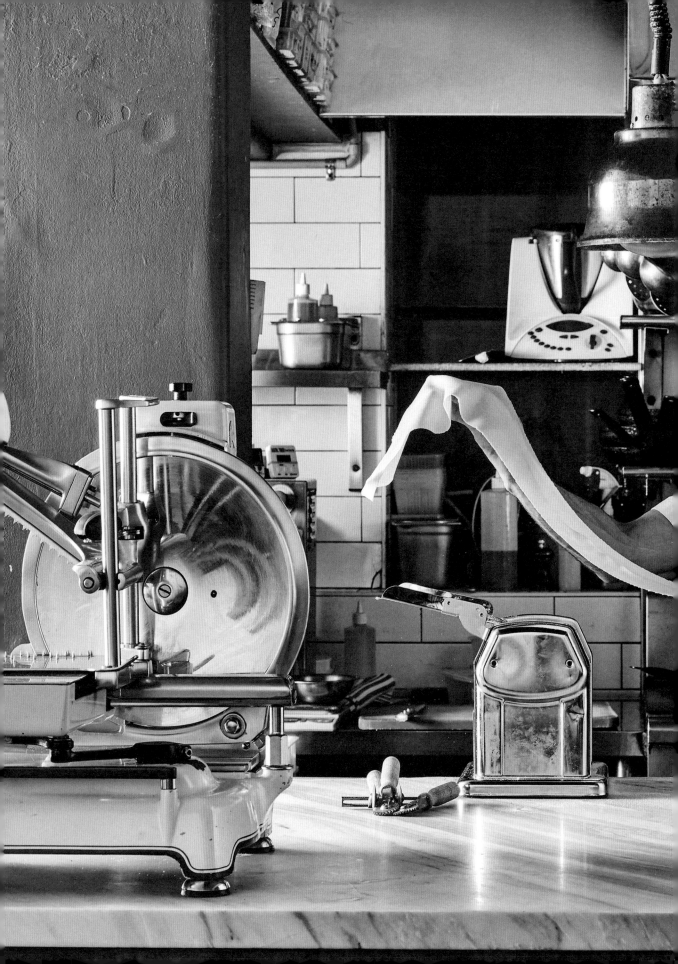

ACKNOWLEDGEMENTS

This cookbook is all about pasta, but Tipo oo is about so much more than that. First and foremost, it is about hospitality, built on the passions and efforts of individuals we have been fortunate to count among our Tipo family. And here, I don't mean myself, Luke or Alberto.

Since our conception, we have been graced with the talents, dedication, enthusiasm and hard work of so many people: from Luke's sister Briony, to Aaron and Alice, whose design vision of honesty and simplicity was the founding principle not just of the Tipo brand but our entire vibe; to Luke's Dad, who built and fitted out the whole thing on a shoestring budget; to all of our front-of-house heroes, forever making Tipo be Tipo.

Then there are our chefs, past and present, who make sure every grain of our Tipo oo flour does what we need it to do, and every strand of pasta is cooked to what we believe is the right kind of al dente.

I grew up close to nature, enveloped in an intrinsic farm-to-table ethos that stemmed from our way of life. But in Melbourne, surrounded by farmers, fishermen, growers and importers so passionate and knowledgeable about their products, I have been able to take this to the next level, and to truly understand the importance of this community of producers and suppliers. Without them we wouldn't exist.

And, of course, there is Luke, the most driven person that anyone could ever meet, and so much of the reason why moving forward, growing and being inspired comes easily for me.

In Alberto, I have a true compatriot – as much as our bouncing of ideas often makes us look like we are arguing or never really agreeing, our end result invariably makes us both smile.

Then there is my actual family. That Anne is still there by my side after this crazy whirlwind of a journey is more a testament to her faith, support and love than anything for which I have been responsible.

Lastly, this book would not have been possible if I hadn't met Jane: she's been a guiding and driving force behind this since we first mooted the idea years ago. As for the recipes, they wouldn't be nearly so fluid, easy to follow or bulletproof without the editing and expert guidance of Alison and Virginia. Thank you to Michael Harden for the words; to Mark and Lee for the stunning photography and styling; and to Andy and Megan for designing and beautifully putting it together.

INDEX

finger limes
finger lime dressing 60
Spaghetti with marron & finger
lime 60
fish
cured rainbow trout 47
Fish stock 216
Midnight spaghetti 156
preparing sardines 164
saffron stock 50
Spaghetti with cured rainbow
trout, mussels & tomato
butter 47
Spaghettini with red mullet &
onion-anchovy sauce 50–1
Squid ink tagliolini with
calamari 44
Stuffed sardines 164
see also anchovies, eel
flour, quality and ratio 21
Focaccia 212–13
frangipane 193
frisee *see* endive
fusilli 28
Fusilli al ferretto with
puttanesca sauce 106–7

G

garlic
Chargrilled broccolini with
bagna cauda & almonds 173
wild garlic emulsion 127
Wild garlic risotto with crab &
preserved lemon 12
garganelli 30
Garganelli with ragu Bolognese
136–7
Globe artichokes with almond
puree & pangrattato 167
gnocchi 30
gnocchi dough 89
Gnocchi with duck & porcini
ragu 88–9
gnocco fritto 179

H

hazelnuts *see* nuts
Herb oil 206
House dressing 208

I

infused oils *see* oils

J

Juniper pappardelle with wild boar
ragu 62–3
juniper–raspberry pasta dough 62

K

kale *see* cavolo nero

L

Lasagne 134
leeks
Octopus with leek & salsa
verde 174–5
Vegetable stock 218
lemons
almond puree 167
Cannelloni with smoked
eggplant & ricotta 103
Fish stock 216
Globe artichokes with almond
puree & pangrattato 167
Lobster risotto with zucchini
flowers 128–9
Mayonnaise 210
Nettle & pink peppercorn
risotto 122
Orecchiette with cime di rapa,
anchovy & pangrattato
146–7
Pangrattato 211
smoked eel mayonnaise 168
Vitello 'anquillato' with capers
& parsley 168
Wild garlic risotto with crab &
preserved lemon 127
linguine 27
Linguine with vongole &
smoked cherry tomatoes 57
Lobster risotto with zucchini
flowers 128–9

M

mandarins
Mandarin panna cotta with oat
crumble 194
mandarin puree 194

marinade 180
marron: Spaghetti with marron &
finger lime 60
mascarpone
mascarpone cream 189
Tipomisu 188–9
Master Pasta Dough 23–4
Mayonnaise 210
mayonnaise, smoked eel 168
Midnight spaghetti 156
mousse, parmesan 162
mousse, White chocolate & fig leaf,
with berries 196
mozzarella: Buffalo mozzarella
with pistachio pesto & gnocco
fritto 179
mushrooms
Cocoa paccheri with pine
mushrooms & pine nuts
76–7
duck ragu 88
Fermented mushroom risotto
124–5
Gnocchi with duck & porcini
ragu 88–9
mushroom stock 124
Vegetable stock 218
mussels: Spaghetti with cured
rainbow trout, mussels & tomato
butter 47

N

Napoli tomato sauce 219
nettles
Nettle & pink peppercorn
risotto 122
Nettle oil 207
nettle puree 122
Paccheri with rabbit ragu &
nettle oil 84–5
picking 122
nuts
almond puree 167
Buffalo mozzarella with
pistachio pesto & gnocco
fritto 179
buying hazelnuts 54
buying pistachios 179
Chargrilled broccolini with
bagna cauda & almonds 173
Cocoa paccheri with pine
mushrooms & pine nuts
76–7

Published in 2024 by Murdoch Books,
an imprint of Allen & Unwin

Murdoch Books Australia
Cammeraygal Country
83 Alexander Street
Crows Nest NSW 2065
Phone: +61 (0)2 8425 0100
murdochbooks.com.au
info@murdochbooks.com.au

For corporate orders and custom publishing,
contact our business development team at
salesenquiries@murdochbooks.com.au

Publisher: Jane Willson
Editorial manager: Virginia Birch, Loran McDougall
Head of creative: Megan Pigott
Designer: Andy Warren
Illustrator: Robin Cowcher
Writer: Michael Harden
Editor: Alison Cowan
Photographer: Mark Roper
Stylist: Lee Blaylock
Production director: Lou Playfair

Murdoch Books UK
Ormond House
26–27 Boswell Street
London WC1N 3JZ
Phone: +44 (0) 20 8785 5995
murdochbooks.co.uk
info@murdochbooks.co.uk

Murdoch Books acknowledges the Traditional Owners
of the Country on which we live and work. We pay our
respects to all Aboriginal and Torres Strait Islander
Elders, past and present.

OVEN GUIDE: You may find cooking times vary
depending on the oven you are using. For conventional
ovens, as a general rule, set the oven temperature to
20°C (35°F) higher than indicated in the recipe.

TABLESPOON MEASURES: We have used 20 ml
(4 teaspoon) tablespoon measures. If you are using a
15 ml (3 teaspoon) tablespoon add an extra teaspoon
of the ingredient for each tablespoon specified.

Text © Andreas Papadakis 2024
The moral right of the author has been asserted.
Design © Murdoch Books 2024
Photography © Mark Roper 2024
Illustrations © Robin Cowcher 2024

10 9 8 7 6 5 4 3 2 1

FSC
www.fsc.org

MIX
Paper | Supporting
responsible forestry
FSC® C008047

ISBN 978 1 92261 650 0

NATIONAL
LIBRARY
OF AUSTRALIA

A catalogue record for this
book is available from the
National Library of Australia

A catalogue record for this book is available from the
British Library

Colour reproduction by Splitting Image Colour Studio
Pty Ltd, Wantirna, Victoria
Printed by C&C Offset Printing Co. Ltd., China

REMEMBER
it's only pasta.

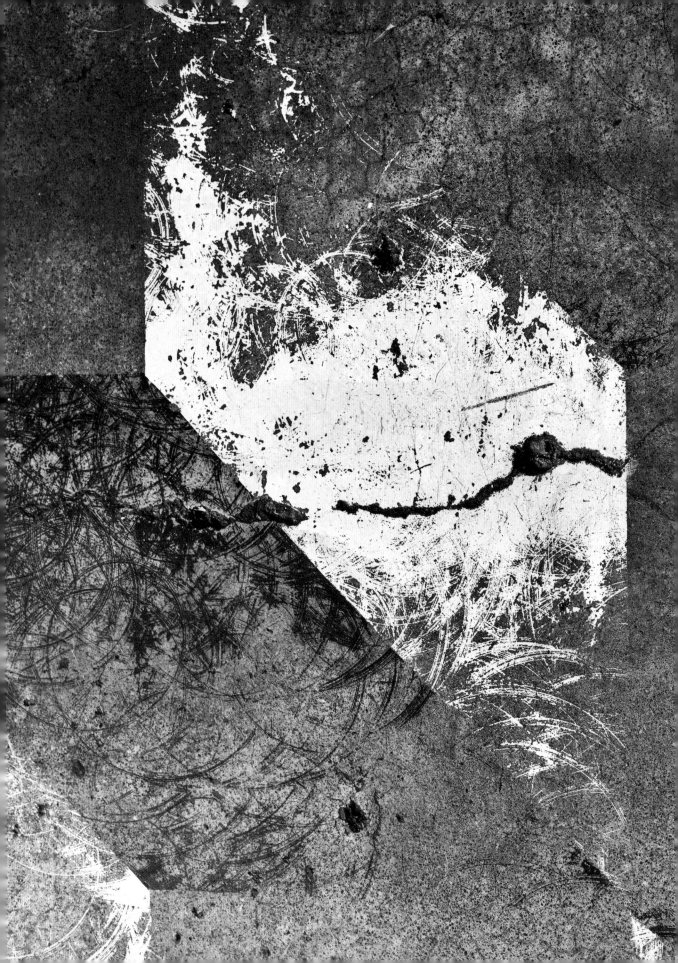